Minute Musings

Spontaneous Combustions of Thought

Volume Two

Daily Inspirational Messages
with
Scriptural References to Jesus Christ

compiled by

Philip M. Hudson

Copyright 2015 by Philip M. Hudson.
The book author retains sole copyright to his contributions to this book.

Published 2015.
Printed in the United States of America.

All rights reserved.

No portion of this book may be reproduced, stored in a retrieval system, or transmitted in any form or by any means – electronic, mechanical, photocopy, recording, scanning, or other – except for brief quotations in critical reviews or articles, without the prior written permission of the author.

ISBN 978-1-937862-99-2

Library of Congress Control Number 2015909163

This book was published by BookCrafters
Parker, Colorado.
bookcrafters@comcast.net

This book may be ordered from
www.bookcrafters.net
and other online bookstores.

Minute Musings

Spontaneous Combustions of Thought

Volume Two

Daily Inspirational Messages
with
Scriptural References to Jesus Christ

Preface

Introduction..1

366 Inspirational Messages with Scriptural References to Jesus Christ........................5

Appendix One: Chronological List (Volume Two)....................................373

Appendix Two: Alphabetical List (Volume Two)......................................389

Appendix Three: Comprehensive Alphabetical Master List....................403

Appendix Four: Numerical List by Body of Scripture..............................463

About the Author..467

Also by the Author..469

Preface

Part of my motivation for compiling these three volumes has been the desire to create an opportunity for family groups to be "on the same page" in relation to at least one aspect of their religious experience. If every participant spent less than a minute reading a particular day's inspirational message about the Savior, perhaps the seeds that were planted could be nurtured in their minds as the day played out. Maybe knowing that they were pondering the same thoughts about the Savior, at the same time, would help to draw them closer together as a family. Perhaps they could even establish an on-going dialogue, as they shared with each other their unique perspectives relating to the daily topic of discussion.

I could have done an Internet search and come up with a pretty good list of the different scriptural references to the Savior. But going through the scriptures on my own voyage of discovery has been a wonderful experience. I did it lightning-fast, to be sure, but I really enjoyed it, and as I traveled through history page by page, it all seemed to tie together in an interesting way that had eluded me in the past.

I was also amazed to discover anew the profound witness of the Savior that permeates the Standard Works. It seemed that in every chapter, there were references to Him that I had somehow previously overlooked. It may be obvious to you, but I had not heretofore recognized the overwhelming testament of Jesus Christ that is found throughout the scriptures.

We are quite familiar with some of His name-titles and descriptions, and they easily roll off our tongues. We use them in our thoughts, prayers, testimonies, lessons, and conversations. Others are less obvious, but as I pondered them, I gained a greater appreciation of what may have been going through the minds of the prophets who recorded them as they received impressions and revelations. I began to understand that they had employed particular terminology in order to convey powerfully relevant messages. In just a few words, there were sermons to be studied. I realized that as we usually describe the Savior, we scarcely plumb the depths of His personality, and our gratitude for His mission only penetrates the surface layers of His divinity. I learned that I am only beginning to feel the impact His life has had on me, and to acknowledge its subtle influence on every aspect of my existence.

Finally, I thought of the observation of Nephi, who wrote: "We talk of Christ, we rejoice in Christ, we preach of Christ, we prophesy of Christ, and we write according to our prophecies, that our children may know to what source they may look for a remission of their sins." (2 Nephi 25:26). In the First Book of Nephi alone, he referred to the Savior in many ways, including The Lord God Almighty, The Messiah, The Lord our God, The God of Israel, The Savior of the World, The Lamb of God, Our Redeemer, The Son of the Everlasting God, The Son of the Eternal Father, The Eternal God, The God of Israel, and The Holy One of Israel, to name just a few. Each of these descriptions suggests that Nephi had more than just a superficial relationship with Jesus Christ. It would be great if these volumes could help us to know the Savior as he did.

Introduction

"What Think Ye of Christ?"
(Matthew 22:42).

This book is about our Lord and Savior Jesus Christ, His doctrine, and our application of His teachings in the modern world. Within its pages you will find 366 references to Him that are found in the scriptures, one for every day of the year, including February 29. Each includes a few lines of related text, intended to prompt you to remember Him throughout the day. The thoughts are intentionally brief, designed to provide an incentive for you to maintain the habit of consistent reflection, and to give you plenty of wiggle-room to thoughtfully expand upon the topic of the day, as you are moved upon by the Spirit to do so.

As I read the scriptures in my preparation to write the book, I was introduced to hundreds of intriguing nuances of expression by the prophets who testified of the Savior. Many familiar name-titles immediately caught my attention, as they undoubtedly have yours. I quickly realized that in these cases, holy men of God had received inspiration to use specific words that dramatically captured the essence of divine character traits that were germane to their related messages. These, I realized, must be revelatory name-titles that were intentionally and inseparably intertwined with prophetic insight and instruction, and I was amazed at how complimentary and mutually supportive the two seemed to be. I also found that the prophets tended to repeat themselves and each other, regularly borrowing favorite name-tiles from their contemporaries and from earlier writings, either quoting them verbatim or enhancing them slightly when they wanted to emphasize the threads of commonality that were woven into the foundation principles and doctrines that accompanied inspired instruction.

In fact, I discovered that there existed an amazing consistency and harmony betweeen the expressions of the prophets in the four Standard Works (the Bible, the Book of Mormon, the Doctrine and Covenants, and the Pearl of Great Price). As one would expect, all of those who contributed their own personal testament of Christ to these texts had a solid grasp of the divine nature of the Savior's mission, and manipulated language as an art form in order to be clear and persuasive, to relate more personally to their callings, to be true to their times, to touch the mystic chords of brotherhood that exist between all people, and to effectively address the spiritual needs of those whom they served.

In many cases, the Savor was portrayed in moving terms that contributed significantly to doctrinal and historical relevancy; however, the inclusion of these word-pictures in the scriptures seemed to be palpably less critical to the overall impact of the messages of the prophets and their reception by the people. These I would characterize as descriptions, rather than as name-titles. My testimony of the divine authenticity of the scriptures was strengthened with my realization that both name-titles and descriptions of the Savior reveal His nature in a new and refreshing light as they introduce multiple layers of His personality to our understanding, and as they clarify the applicability of holy writ to our circumstances. Name-titles and descriptions are sprinkled throughout the pages of this book like powdered sugar over a mouth-watering dessert, in no particular order or structure, although I have tried to make each one apropos to the topic at hand. The purpose of their inclusion is to invite the Spirit, add sweet savor, and enhance your benfit from, and enjoyment of, Minute Musings. As Peter Pan told Wendy: "All you need is faith, trust, and a little bit of pixie dust, and you can fly!"

The book does not pretend to comprise an exhaustive list. As a matter of fact, I initially envisioned creating just one volume, but as I became more heavily involved in my investigation of the scriptures, it soon became apparent that I would need to expand the scope of my efforts to at least three volumes. The appendices that follow the body of the text are designed to help you to quickly and easily navigate your way to your favorite name-titles and descriptions. They also extend an invitation to discover on your own many references to the Savior with which you may not have been familiar. Following Appendix Three are several pages that summon you to literally fill in the blanks with additional citations describing the nature and character of Jesus Christ. Doing so should personalize the book for you, strengthen your faith, reinforce your testimony of the Savior, and contribute to your more profound appreciation and application of the scriptures. Perhaps, at some point, there will be a need for a fourth, and even a fifth, volume that could represent our collaborative efforts.

Coming up with the list was actually the easy part. Writing the commentary was more challenging. I am sure I mis-stated myself more than once, or only awkwardly described a concept here or there. When you find a glaring example of my weakness in writing, remember that my age entitles me to a free pass every now and then. Give me the benefit of the doubt, and allow me to have a senior moment. Use my feeble effort as a springboard to launch your own more articulate interpretation of the signification of the particular name-title or description under consideration.

As you flip through Minute Musings, the physical symmetry of the layout of each page should be immediately apparent. When I put pen to paper, so to speak, I was struck by the need to bring balance and equilibrium to the thoughts that had crystalized in my mind. Striving to create artistry and proportion in phraseology was challenging, but it helped me to achieve a sense of stability that was at the same time refreshing and even stimulating. I believe that when we think of the Savior, and particularly when we record our impressions of Him, either for ourselves or for the benefit of others, He deserves our very best efforts, and for me, that meant creating something of not only intellectual and spiritual value, but also of aesthetic appeal.

I do know this. The Savior is the rudder of my ship, guiding me past unseen rocks and reefs. He is my helm, holding steady when winds of adversity blow. He is my telltale, alerting me to impending storms. He is my keel, helping me to move against the current and the wind. He is my mainsheet, holding firmly with just enough pressure to prevent me from capsizing when I am heeled over. He is my safety-line, providing security when my footing is unsure and the foaming sea is streaming across my deck. He is my compass, showing me the way, especially when the course is unclear. He is my chart, warning me of hidden dangers. He is my barometer, alerting me to impending storms. He is my sextant, orienting me not only to the stars, but also to eternity. He is my lookout, standing as my sentinel when I am distracted by trivial concerns. He holds the line that trails in my wake, offering safety when I fall overboard. He is the wind that fills my sails.

I testify of His ante-mortal existence, and of His foreordination to be the Redeemer of the world. The scriptures speak of His relationship with the Father, and of His divine investiture of authority. His appearances to His servants throughout history were many. The Book of Mormon, particularly, explains His condescension in taking a mortal body. Thus, I can better understand His temptations, and the power, might, dominion, and authority that typified His experience on the earth.

In His baptism, He demonstrated by example the way for me to follow. In His ministry, He taught the truths of the Gospel in simplicity. In the Garden of Gethsemane, He demonstrated His fortitude and compassion. The crucifixion, then, was only an apostrophe; His death but a pause to allow us to re-focus our attention on His resurrection and ascension into heaven.

He is my Advocate with the Father, and the Bread of Life. He is the Cornerstone of my creation, the Foundation of my existence. He is the Creator of worlds without number, and the Deliverer of the Covenant to all the children of our Father.

He is Emmanuel: truly, in Him God is with me. The Firstborn of the Spirit Children of the Father, He is Perfect in every detail. He is the Good Shepherd, and the Judge of both the quick and the dead. As Lord, King, and Jehovah, He has all power to act as our Mediator and as the Messenger of the Covenant.

The Lamb of God, He is the Messiah, the Anointed One, and my Redeemer. He is my Rock, and my Savior, the Only Begotten Son of God in the flesh. He is the Son of Man of Holiness, and my Second Comforter.

When He returns, it will be in the clouds. He will be accompanied by the Church of the Firstborn, and His Second Coming will usher in His Millennial Reign. For a thousand years, His Gospel will penetrate every soul and burn brightly in every bosom. I hope we will all be there to savor the experience together.

January 1

The Lord, even the Savior
(Doctrine & Covenants 133:25)

Because the
world goes to such
great lengths to throw us off
balance, even those of us who are
Born Again require constant and repetitive
encouragement from **The Lord, even the Savior**,
to strengthen our resolve to steady our course
so that we might move forward in
an endless progression.

January 2

The Shadow of Thing to Come
(Colossians 2:17)

We
cannot
afford to sleep
at our posts, or even
to doze off every now and
then. If we allow complacency
to overcome us, we will be swept
over the precipice of destruction. **The
Shadow of Things to Come** ignites our
imagination, stimulates our capacity
for purposeful, constructive, and
affirmative action, and helps
us to maintain our poise
and balance.

January 3

Jesus, the Mediator of the New Covenant
(Doctrine & Covenants 107:19)

In our journey through mortality, **Jesus, the Mediator of the New Covenant**, strengthens and blesses us, but not necessarily with telestial toys that might take us on detours leading away from the familiarity and steadiness of the strait and narrow path. Nor will He coddle us by making our way easy, lest we be pacified into a false sense of carnal security and lose our forward momentum. The constant force of gravity exerted by our uphill path of progress very subtly counteracts the negative effects of complacency that might otherwise lead to a disastrous free-fall from faith.

January 4

The Lord Jesus Christ, the Son of the Father
(2 Nephi 11:32)

As we
learn to balance our
lives, **The Lord Jesus Christ,
the Son of the Father**, subtly fortifies
us, and gives us opportunities to be engaged
in good causes. He has endowed us with untapped
capacity. With His nurturing assistance, we can align
ourselves with His limitless power to avoid telestial traffic
jams. He helps us to work out our salvation with fear
and trembling. He nudges us to move out of our
comfort zones into the stimulating environment
of service. He even asks us to confront those
uncomfortable circumstances that ask us
to surrender our agency to powers
that are higher than
ourselves.

January 5

God
the Eternal Father
(Doctrine & Covenants 20:77)

Our **God
the Eternal Father** has
exhorted us to drink copiously and
unceasingly from the fountain of truth
in order to slake our thirst for principles that
gyroscopically orient us to the eternities. He
understands the difference between celestial
sureties that are represented by eternal
progression, and telestial tendencies
that are characterized by physical
laws such as entropy.

January 6

The
Messenger of Salvation
(Doctrine & Covenants 93:8)

The Messenger of Salvation provides the only viable alternative to Satan's crushing ability to negatively influence our lives. The stipulation is that after we realize we have been disobedient, we must go through the process of repentance. We recognize our transgression, experience remorse, renounce the self-defeating behavior, resolve to do better, make restitution where possible, and then do our part to establish a reconciliation with the Spirit, and ultimately receive a remission of our sin.

January 7

The Christ, the Eternal God
(2 Nephi 26:12)

Opposition allows us to gauge the success of our efforts to internalize the provisions of the Plan, and gives us a sense of how we are doing in our labors to consciously and energetically participate in purposeful programs of personal progress that have the unqualified endorsement of **The Christ, the Eternal God**.

January 8

Man of Holiness is My Name
(Moses 7:35)

Too often, we
satisfy ourselves with
a brief glimpse of salvation
in a mirror, without ever beholding
our potential, and without ever breaking
free of our enslavement to the upsetting laws
of destructive behavior. We behold our face in a
glass, darkly. However, when we personalize
the **Man of Holiness**, and recognize in our
own countenances the very prototype of
His image, our resolve is quickened,
or given vitality, to pattern our
lives after His example.

January 9

God
of Glory
(Moses 1:20)

Perhaps
we should budget our
time as carefully as we budget
our money. Concentrating on things that
really matter endows us with special powers
to manage the gift of time. We learn to make time
with diligence, take time with discipline, spend time
with thoughtfulness, find time with insight, invest time
with wisdom, and share time with pleasure. Turning our
attention to the weightier matters of the law gives us a sense
of independence, as we learn something new every day.
Embracing the learning style of the **God of Glory** can
open our hearts and our minds to a breathtaking
expansion of understanding. When we create
time in our busy lives to enjoy the Spirit,
we discover within ourselves His
design, that becomes
our norm.

January 10

The Rock That is Higher Than I
(Psalms 62:1)

The promises that bind me to **The Rock That is Higher Than I** solidify a personal relationship with the Savior that allows Him to bestow upon me and my loved ones individually-tailored and specific blessings. I receive the right to guidance from the Holy Ghost that is crafted to meet my needs. My wife and daughters receive the rights and privileges, and the blessings and responsibilities, that are related to femininity. My sons receive the right to hold and exercise the priesthood. Our extended family receives the promise of eternal life in the Celestial Kingdom of our Father.

January 11

The
Stem of Jesse
(Isaiah 11:1)

The four
fundamental forces of
nature are gravity, electromagnetism,
the strong force, and the weak force. They
hold the universe together. Gravity, in particular,
helps to ground us to **The Stem of Jesse**, and to trace
our lineage back to our roots. It orients us to our
temporal environment, while giving us just
enough latitude to be able to sense the
influence of a steady pull from
the eternal world.

January 12

Prophet
(Deuteronomy 18:15)

Counsel from
our **Prophet** allows us
to brush with bold strokes as
we work on our life's portrait, and to
create sweeping swaths of color across very
large canvases. Embracing His artistic tutoring
can motivate us to venture into uncharted territory
where we are blessed with refreshing, stimulating,
unconventional, and unorthodox experiences that
take us beyond the dimensions of height, depth,
or breadth to the realm of spiritual and sensory
delight. His guidance transforms our earthly
home into a thought-provoking studio and
imaginative learning laboratory that
can generate success stories and
turn dreams into reality.

January 13

The
Great Mediator
(2 Nephi 2:28)

When we
are over the hill
we sometimes would
like to use our momentum
to pick up speed. Instead, we
may need to ease off on the throttle
of our expectations, and simply gird up
our loins and take fresh courage, knowing
that it is not ability or inability that is
important, but availability. We
consecrate our efforts to **The
Great Mediator**, and let
Him sort out the
details.

January 14

A Figure for the Time then Present
(Hebrews 9:9)

When we
are anxiously engaged,
we influence more than we
are moved upon by others, we lead
rather than follow, and light candles rather
than cursing the darkness. When it rains, we do
not complain about the weather, but quietly open
up our umbrellas. We don't allow ourselves to get in
the thick of thin things. We stem the tide rather than
allowing ourselves to be passively swept up by it,
we solve problems instead of ignoring them, and
we learn to pay it forward. We realize that the
power to change rests within us, but that
the source of our clean, green, and
renewable energy is **A Figure
for the Time then
Present**.

January 15

A Rock of Offense
to Both the Houses of Israel
(Isaiah 8:14)

To
sustain
real vitality, our
forgiveness needs to
be anchored to the Savior's
Atonement. Our carnal nature
that harbors feelings of revenge,
retaliation, and reprisal is nothing
more than a shadowy reflection of the
rebellion of Lucifer. If our base instincts
are to be restrained, the fire line that is
necessary to contain, control, and
conquer the conflagration of sin
must be supervised by the
**Rock of Offense to
Both the Houses
of Israel**.

January 16

A Stumbling Stone and Rock of Offense
(Romans 9:33)

The divine principle of forgiveness is so alien to our carnal, sensual, and devilish nature, that the devil is helpless to muster an effective counter-attack. Nothing in his arsenal of tricks can combat its power. The best he can do is keep us from the truth, for he knows that the knowledge of our origin and destiny will make us free. The Savior is **A Stumbling Stone and a Rock of Offense** only to those who embrace Satan's opposition to His compassion.

January 17

Messiah, the King of Zion,
the Rock of Heaven
(Moses 7:53)

If
we ever
hope to be able to
successfully deal with the
inequalities of life and escape
the quicksands of self-pity, we must
personalize the lesson of the Atonement.
We must change our nature and become new
creatures in **Messiah, the King of Zion, the
Rock of Heaven**. If necessary, we must
practice in front of a mirror and recite
over and over again until we get
it right: "Father forgive them,
for they know not what
they do." We must
become more
Amish.

January 18

I, God
(Doctrine & Covenants 19:16)

Equilibrium in our lives
necessarily sets the stage for the
exercise of moral agency and dictates
the implementation of other equally important
and co-existing laws. Mercy, in particular, exists to
mitigate the otherwise inevitable consequences resulting
from lives out of balance, and through the Atonement our
journey of progress both in time and in eternity is facilitated.
To hear with our hearts: "**I God**, forgive you. Now go and
sin no more," reverses the disorder and destruction that
is the result of imbalance. Our obedience nurtures the
development of personality traits and behaviors
that are consistent with the symmetry,
stability, and steadiness of the
nature of our Lord and
Savior.

January 19

I am God
(Moses 7:35)

Even
though we
mindlessly toil with
our blood, sweat, and tears,
and sacrifice even those things
that are near and dear to us in order
to obtain telestial treasures, at the last day
the unevenness of the world can only deliver
physical destruction, while steady obedience to
the laws of the Gospel creates opportunities
to progress eternally. How comforting it
is for us to have a personal witness of
the sweetness of the expression:
"Be still, and know that
I am God."

January 20

Christ the Power of God and the Wisdom of God
(1 Corinthians 1:24)

Our destination is well-defined, and if we only half-heartedly seek truth it is because our instability causes us to confuse knowledge for intelligence, and to think that when we are learned we are wise. We must never fail to understand that it is good to be educated, but only if we hearken to God's counsel. Our recognition of **Christ, the Power of God and the Wisdom of God**, kindles our faith and protects our testimonies. It can also save our souls.

January 21

Only Begotten
(Moses 3:18)

The **Only Begotten** of the Father prepares us for "that special moment when we are figuratively tapped on our shoulder and offered a chance to do a very special thing, unique to us and fitted to our talents. What a tragedy if that moment finds us unprepared or unqualified for that which could have been our finest hour."
(Churchill).

January 22

Jesus is
the Very Christ
(2 Nephi 26:12)

The constant and
relentless G-force exerted
by the uphill process of inquiry
that ultimately leads to a testimony that
Jesus is the Very Christ is in contrast to the
casual and carefree coast into complacency that
inevitably takes an uncommitted soul onto a slippery
slope above a personality precipice. Sooner or later, there
will be a sickening free-fall because of the lack of protection
provided by the parachute of Gospel principles. We can
become new creatures in Christ only if we maintain
perfect symmetry, oriented more to the laws of
the eternal world and the guidance of the
Master than to the fickle limitations that
are imposed by the physical world,
and that are the inescapably
destructive consequences
of disproportion.

January 23

I,
The Lord God
(Moses 3:6)

The
physical signs and
symptoms of inflammation
include redness, swelling, pain,
heat, and loss of function. Powerful
inflammatory influences also combine to
contribute to the loss of our virtue. Surprisingly,
diversity may exist within the fold to gyroscopically
orient us to our Divine Center as we deal with spiritual
identity theft. The diversity of the Saints may be defined
by contrast, but it also highlights threads of commonality
that might not be so immediately obvious. Perhaps **The
Lord God** created diversity as a manifestation of the
opposition in all things that is so critical to the
successful implementation of the Plan.
Diveristy just may strengthen our
shared identity as His
offspring.

January 24

Only Begotten, even Jesus Christ
(Moses 7:50)

Stitched right into the
fabric of the Plan of Salvation
is our capacity to endure to the end.
Agency provides us with the choice to do it
either righteously or unrighteously. If we opt for
the latter, we have implicitly accepted the inevitable
negative consequences of sin, which makes endurance
much more painful for us than it would otherwise have
needed to be. However, when we elect to endure in
righteousness, the **Only Begotten, even Jesus
Christ**, will provide us with opportunities
for purposeful and positive action that,
over time, gives even our most
challenging experiences an
exhilarating twist.

January 25

The
Righteous
(Moses 7:47)

We
are grateful for
our diversity. It serves
a purpose by illuminating the
common autobiographical thread
that leads back to our Father in Heaven.
We recognize that there are many mansions in
the kingdom of **The Righteous**, and there is
room in His dominion for Nephites and
Lamanites, Greeks and Romans, Jews
and Gentiles, the rich as well as the
poor, those who are black or
white, and those who are
free or who have been
in bondage to
sin.

January 26

The Lord thy God
(Abraham 2:7)

Disorder
and disobedience
go hand-in-hand. Chaotic
conditions take the rebellious
further and further from the influence
of the Spirit, whose purpose it is to guide
us away from that precipice of destruction to
the more secure sanctuary that abides the stability of
higher laws. Damnation results from activities that block
the channels through which this spiritual power flows.
It is the halt in our progression, because of imbalance
in our lives, that is damning. Righteousness, on
the other hand, welcomes a steadiness that is
accompanied by a reassuring voice that
whispers: "**The Lord thy God**
justifies thy efforts."

January 27

Him that hath Called us to Glory and Virtue
(2 Peter 1:3)

If we try to
conduct our lives
without the liberating
infuence of the Atonement, we
are doomed to suffer in the shadows,
and experience only a dancing light show
punctuated by the flicker of illusions that are
only caricatures of reality. The discrepancy between
our marginalized behavior and the ideals of the Plan
conceived and executed by **Him that hath Called
us to Glory and Virtue** will become so great
that our short-lived pleasure in worldly
ways will surely evaporate as does
the morning dew in the
heat of the day.

January 28

God
of Gods
(Deuteronomy 10:17)

The Merciful
Plan of the **God of Gods**
has been designed to save even
the worst of His children, but only after
they have changed their nature and have
repented, or when they have personally paid
the penalty for their own sins. Those of us who
continue to press forward toward the Tree of Life
experience glimmers of the hope of salvation,
even as we find ourselves in the company
of sinners very much like ourselves who
often feel unworthy and undeserving
of His unconditional love
and His grace.

January 29

God
in the Highest
(Luke 2:14)

When we
are balanced, we
are determined and resolute,
unwavering, decided, dogged, untiring,
indomitable, and even heroic. Balance is the
opposite of fanaticism, when we lose sight of our
objectives but redouble our efforts. To be balanced
is to be zealous, enthusiastic, passionate, fervent,
ardent, and eager in matters pertaining to **God
in the Highest**, versus overzealousness,
wherein we may become obsessive
and even feverish in our
discipleship.

January 30

My God, and your God
(Moses 6:43)

We must be
especially vigilant to
avoid over-zealous desires
that rivet our attention, consume
our energies, and demand our devotion.
If we sit at spiritual stop signs and rev our
engines in neutral, our ability to move ahead
in a partnership with **My God and your God** is
incapacitated. Even if our intentions are good,
we must avoid looking beyond the mark, or
becoming side-tracked or confused by
telestial traffic circles that take us
round and round without
making any forward
progress.

January 31

Prince and a Savior
(Acts 5:31)

Progress is
our recompense
for perseverance, while
salvation is our reward for
surmounting obstacles, and
eternal life is our blessing as we
endure opposition. With the Spirit
balancing our experiences, we become
more comfortable with the perspective
that confirms that Gospel principles
relating to our **Prince and a Savior**
can supersede physical laws
that pertain only to the
temporal world.

February 1

The Son
(Moses 5:15)

There will come
a time in each of our
lives when its meaning
snaps into focus, and we
see things as they really are.
We will experience a state of
balance and symmetry whose
lucidity comes more from the
heart than from the head. In
that state of tranquility, we
will better understand the
true nature of **The Son**
of the Highest.

February 2

The
Eternal God
(Doctrine & Covenants 121:32)

The Eternal God knew beforehand that when we left our first estate, we would be confronted with seemingly contradictory principles relating to His never-ending concern on the one hand, and our promised birthright of agency or free will on the other. To resolve this conundrum, the gift of time was created and then stitched into the Plan as a dimension unique to mortality. "Now it is high time to awake out of sleep," wrote Paul. "For now is our salvation nearer than when we believed." (Romans 13:11). With time on our side, God's parental worry has been addressed without violating the Prime Directive that relates to the preservation of our free will.

February 3

The Father, and the Son, and the Holy Ghost
(3 Nephi 11:27)

In a single
stroke of genius,
**The Father, and the Son,
and the Holy Ghost** harnessed the
power of the quixotic element of time and
apportioned it in discrete seconds, minutes, and
hours, where it could be combined with agency to
generate and sustain spontaneity. The scriptures record
that before the dawn of creation: "The Lord said: Let us go
down. And they went down at the beginning, and they,
that is the Gods, organized and formed the heavens
and the earth." (Abraham 4:1). At the beginning,
the celestial clock was re-set and calibrated on a
temporal scale, whereas its design in the
eternities had been "the Lord's time,
according to the reckoning of
Kolob." (Abraham 3:4).

February 4

The Father and I are One
(3 Nephi 28:10)

The Mortal Messiah, who stands as
our Exemplar, explained: The Father and I
are One. They illustrate the summit of the spirit of
synchronization and harmony that can exist in relationships,
and typify the divine characteristic of joy that accompanies
participation in the grounded approach to rearing children
that is at the core of Their divine center. Perhaps best of all,
Their design teaches us parenting skills that can mitigate
the risk of experiencing the heartbreak of losing our
little ones through either the friendly fire of over-
protection or the damaging consequences of
inattention. As we send them out into the
world to negotiate the minefields of
mortality, any collateral damage
may be kept to a minimum as
they conform to the pattern
of the Plan.

February 5

He Who hath Perfected Forever
them that are Sanctified
(Hebrews 10:14)

Members of the
Church do not enjoy a
monopoly on revelation. Many
of our friends and neighbors believe
there are angels among us, and there are
countless newlyweds who are certain that
their match was made in heaven. Others feel
that they have somehow been touched by angels.
Spiritual promptings, intuitions, and impressions are
more common that many would suspect. These are
feelings that strongly influence black and white,
bond and free, male and female, both Jew and
Gentile, and even the heathen, to move in
positive directions. If we venture beyond
the ministration of angels, however,
we begin to appreciate the special
intimacy that **He Who hath
Perfected Forever them
That are Sanctified**
enjoys with His
people.

February 6

He
Who Liveth
(Doctrine & Covenants 110:4)

There are many who eat,
drink, and make merry, putting the
inevitable out of their minds, and dulling
their senses with the narcotics of immediate
gratification and deferred consequences. They
roll the dice on the assumption that heaven can wait.
The problem with that flawed perspective is that it leads
to faulty perception and impaired judgment. In real life,
things just don't work that way. The older we get, the
more we realize that **He Who Liveth** can't wait any
more than heaven could, because, just as He
is, we are already living in eternity. "This
life is the time…to prepare to meet
God." (Alma 34:32).

February 7

The
Eternal Judge
(Moroni 10:34)

Living water is
so crucial to our well-being
that our Lord **The Eternal Judge** has
provided a means for the construction of
a conduit that can penetrate solid limestone, as
it were, so that it may freely flow into our lives. At
great effort, an unobstructed channel may be chiseled
through the accretions of age, rough exteriors, and our
stony nature, with the tools of obedience, charity,
prayer, hope, works, and other healthy lifestyle
choices. Our access to living water is created
when we act on our faith by being honest,
true, chaste, benevolent, virtuous,
kind, and in doing good
to others.

February 8

The Eternal Father of Heaven and Earth
(Mosiah 15:4)

The Eternal Father of Heaven and Earth is the universal life-force for good that is the hope of the world. Isaiah described Him with these words: "For unto us a child is born, unto us a son is given: and the government shall be upon his shoulder: and his name shall be called Wonderful, Counsellor, the Mighty God, the Everlasting Father, the Prince of Peace." (Isaiah 9:6). "The Lord be with you" is an ancient salutation and blessing traditionally used by clergy. In modern vernacular, one might say: "May the Force be with you." As Yoda explained: "My ally is the Force. Its energy surrounds us and binds us. Luminous beings are we. You must feel the force around you, everywhere."

February 9

The
Supreme Being
(Doctrine & Covenants 104:7)

When we feel the pressure to
make signifiant withdrawals from our
spiritual bank accounts, we can still enjoy the
blessing of receiving pennies from heaven. These
come in various forms. First, **The Supreme Being** will
give us "knowledge by the unspeakable gift of the Holy
Ghost." (D&C 121:26). He does not generally give us Susan
B. Anthony or Sacajawea dollars, or even quarters, dimes, or
nickels. Instead, He dispenses the smallest denominations
possible in a currency of faith, nurturing our testimonies
with "precept upon precept; line upon line; here a
little, and there a little." (Isaiah 28:10). As the
accumulation of these coins replenishes
our piggy banks, we increase in
wisdom and in stature, and
in favor with God.

February 10

The
God of Heaven
(Moses 7:28)

Wherever
it may be found, all
truth can be circumscribed into
one whole, and the Merciful Plan of the
Great Creator, or **The God of Heaven**, is the
Holy Grail of religious doctrine. It is the spiritual
equivalent of physics' elusive theory of everything.
But it is even more comprehensive than the Unified
Field Theory that hopes to explain the universe by
bringing together the primal forces of nature
into one grand equation. The Plan defines
our place in the cosmos by putting our
humanity and our divine potential
in juxtaposition. By doing so,
our existence is given
substance, meaning,
and purpose.

February 11

The God of this People of Israel
(Acts 13:17)

There are
no privileged frames
of reference. The galaxies
are imbedded in time and imprinted
upon a space whose fabric is constantly
expanding. When we ask: "Where and when
did the creation take place?" the answer must be
everywhere and forever. The universe may, in fact, be
warped through time and space into other dimensions,
expanding like a balloon, and creating in every instant
more space. It seems plausible that **The God of this
People Israel** would utilize the laws of physics to
accomplish His purposes within the framework
of eternal laws that occasionally supersede our
familiar temporal guidelines. This may help
to explain why He told Joseph that He
would one day reveal "things which
have passed, and hidden things
which no man knew, things of
the earth, by which it was
made, and the purpose
and the end thereof."
(D&C 101:33).

February 12

The Head of the Corner
(1 Peter 2:7)

The Head of the Corner has provided us with tools that relate to healthy and provident living, and that nurture the dependent relationship between obedience to the commandments and physical and spiritual well-being. He knew that "when health is absent, wisdom cannot reveal itself, culture cannot become manifest, strength cannot fight, and intelligence cannot be applied." (Heraclitus). "They that wait upon the Lord," however, "shall renew their strength. They shall mount up with wings as eagles. They shall run, and not be weary, and they shall walk, and not faint." (Isaiah 40:31).

February 13

The Eternal Father
(Doctrine & Covenants 20:77)

The Eternal Father has used "that for which all virtue now is sold, and almost every vice, almighty gold" as a powerful symbolic tool. (Ben Jonson). While our desire for gold typifies a flaw in our character, the image of the bright, shiny metal also describes the purity that turns our attention to the inestimable worth of the Celestial Kingdom. Gold that has been heated in the crucible of the refiner's fire is a dazzling white, and when the earth attains its celestial glory, its streets will be pure gold, as it were, a transparent glass, even a Urim and Thummim.

February 14

The Very Christ
(2 Nephi 26:12)

In the "Star Trek: The Next Generation" episode entitled "Where Silence Has Lease," Captain Jean Luc Picard explains: "Considering the marvelous complexity of the universe, its clockwork perfection, its balances of this against that, such as matter, energy, gravitation, time, and dimension, I believe that our existence must go beyond Euclidean or other practical measuring systems, and that it is part of a reality beyond what we now understand." At its center dwells **The Very Christ**, and the Restoration testifies that He may be known.

February 15

Him Who has Granted Salvation unto His People
(Mosiah 15:18)

Walking in the light of
of the Gospel endows us with
a greater capacity to love **Him Who
has Granted Salvation unto His People**.
Enlightenment dissipates the cobwebs of doubt,
smooths out the rough edges of our testimonies, builds
our self-confidence to tackle tough questions, and provides
the self-assurance we need to use our agency appropriately.
Light may bestow upon us the gifts of peace and a clear
conscience, illuminating eternally valid principles as
the ultimate measure of truth. It exerts a liberating
influence as it frees us from fear, doubt, worry,
ignorance, despair, apprehension, timidity,
and unsteadiness. Light can empower
us to keep that which we hold sacred
safe from those who scurry about
in the shadows and threaten
to ransack our treasury.

February 16

The Lord,
the Redeemer of all Men
(Alma 28:8)

The soothing
administration of
light therapy is similar
to a deep-tissue massage that
strengthens our core, stimulates our
fast-twitch muscle fibers, and increases
our elasticity and flexibility. It channels
our energy, warms up our juices, and
gets them flowing. We walk in the
light to illuminate the doorway
to heaven, beyond which we
will discover **The Lord**,
the Redeemer of
all Men.

February 17

The Lion of
the Tribe of Judah
(Revelation 5:5)

It is
our righteous
desires that shape
our resolve to create a
reduction sauce of spiritual
energy that is pleasing to our
palate. When we can taste the savory
principles of eternal life, we have set the
table for **The Lion of the Tribe of Judah** to
sit down with us to determine a strategy
to meet the challenges that would
have otherwise been barriers to
our personal progress.

February 18

Majesty on High
(Hebrews 1:3)

"The stars fade away, the sun himself grows dim with age, and nature sinks in years; but thou shalt flourish in immortal youth, unhurt amidst the war of elements, the wreck of matter, and the crash of worlds." (Joseph Addison, "Cato"). We look forward to our eternal destiny, never forgetting that we are the spiritually begotten sons and daughters of **Majesty on High**.

February 19

Majesty
(Hebrews 8:1)

Those of us who
have been lucky enough to
see "the rising moon break out
of the clouds at midnight, have been
present like archangels at the creation
of light and of the world." (Emerson).
We have been witness to the work
of the **Majesty** Who rules both
in the heavens and on earth,
Who first spoke the words:
"Let there be light."
(Genesis 1:3).

February 20

The Master of the Vineyard
(Jacob 5:7)

"But you were always a good man of business, Jacob." said Scrooge. "Business!" cried the ghost, wringing its hands again. "Mankind was my business. The common welfare was my business; charity, mercy, forbearance, and benevolence were all my business. The dealings of my trade were but a drop of water in the comprehensive ocean of my business." (Dickens, "A Christmas Carol").
The Master of the Vineyard is ever about His business.

February 21

Omegus, even
Jesus Christ your Lord
(Doctrine & Covenants 95:17)

The
only payment
that is required of you
to obtain forgiveness is your
broken heart and contrite spirit.
The end of your deliverance is **Omegus,
even Jesus Christ your Lord**. Though you will
forever be in His service, you are not in bondage to
Him. He never intended that you live out your days
in a debtor's prison. On the contrary, His Atonement
frees you from the burden of unresolved sin and
entitles you to enjoy the liberating influence of
His companionship when your faith has led
you to repentance and baptism, and
you have then received the gift
of the Holy Ghost.

February 22

The Mediator between God and Men
(1 Timothy 2:5)

The Mediator between God and Men knows that happiness is the purpose of our existence, and will be the end thereof, if we follow the path that leads to it. All that we have to do is be faithful, virtuous, upright, holy, and keep His commandments with exactness.

February 23

Alphus
(Doctrine & Covenants 95:17)

If we
could peer into the
infinite and fathomless
expanse of the universe,
we would sense that before
Wise Men followed a star to
Bethlehem, before the rise of
civilization, before the world
took its present form, before
there were days and nights
or seasons, before there
was life itself on the
earth, there would
be **Alphus**, the
Creator of all
things.

February 24

The Life of Men and the Light of Men
(Doctrine & Covenants 93:9)

He is
our Mentor,
our Exemplar,
our Mediator, our
Deliverer, our King, our
Rock, our Fortress, our
Lord, **The Life of
Men and the
Light of
Men**.

February 25

The Rock
of their Salvation
(Jacob 7:25)

When the
last of the Apostles
fell asleep, the heavens
withdrew, allowing ignorance to
move into the void. Both wisdom and
understanding forsook the sons of Adam
and the daughters of Eve. Darkness filled the
land and the world became a confusing and a
forbidding place. The legions of Satan blinded
the eyes of the children of God to **The Rock of
their Salvation**, poisoned their hearts, and
closed their minds. Perplexity prevailed
until the breaking dawn of a day of
restoration and renewal allowed
the earth to be enveloped
in glorious light.

February 26

The Light which Shineth in Darkness
(Doctrine & Covenants 6:21)

He is **The Light which Shineth in Darkness**.
We see its warm glow in His Gospel,
and find its source in revelation from above.
"If any man preach any other Gospel unto
you than that ye have received,
let him be accursed."
(Galatians 1:9).

February 27

King
of Glory
(Psalms 24:7)

It is the
manifest destiny of
the disciples of Christ to
kindle a fire that will burn so
brightly and with such clarity and
intensity that it will cleanse and purify
the earth and all that lies thereon,
in a final preparation for it
to receive its rightful
King of Glory.

February 28

(Him Who) Appears
in the Presence of God for Us
(Hebrews 9:24)

To be
valiant, noble,
and courageous
in the testimony of
Him Who **Appears in
the Presence of God for
Us**, is to take His side on
every issue, believe as
He believes, think as
He does, speak with
His authority, and
do just what He
would do.

February 29

Him which Delivereth us
from the Wrath to Come
(1 Thessalonians 1:10)

We
enjoy the
quiet sanctuary of
the Spirit, overcome the
enemies of our progression,
and avoid the harsh realities of
Judgment Day, through **Him
which Delivereth us from
the Wrath to Come.**

March 1

The Everlasting Father
(Isaiah 9:6)

No matter what our individual circumstances may be, we must ultimately acknowledge the sobering reality of the overarching supremacy and all-encompassing influence of **The Everlasting Father**.

March 2

God Manifest in the Flesh
(1 Timothy 3:16)

When the
Messiah was born as
God Manifest in the Flesh,
He revealed His character to all
who had eyes to see and ears to hear.
He knew that in order to understand
ourselves, we would first need
to correctly comprehend
His nature.

March 3

Him Who ever Liveth to Make Intercession
(Hebrews 7:25)

Each of
us wears a coat
of many colors, and
our love for **Him Who ever
Liveth to Make Intercession**
for us is reflected by each thread
in the fabric of our being, that
makes up the vibrant
tapestry of our
souls.

March 4

He is True, and Teaches the Way of God in Truth
(Matthew 22:6)

We
cannot
mold Him
into an idea god
to suit our decadent
lifestyle. **He is True,
and Teaches the
Way of God in
Truth.**

March 5

He that Cometh
in the Name of the Lord
(Matthew 21:9)

"Who are these young ones growing tall, growing strong, like silver trees against the storm; who will not bend with the wind or the change, but stand to fight the world alone? These are the few, the warriors saved for Saturday, to come the last day of the world." (Doug Stewart). These are the dauntless disciples of the Chosen One **that Cometh in the Name of the Lord**.

March 6

He
that is Holy
(Revelation 3:7)

The divine personality traits of our Lord and Savior Jesus Christ are reflected in the covenants we make with **He that is Holy**. Because He is moral, He gives us the covenant of chastity. He is a righteous steward, and provides us with the Law of Consecration. He has charity for all men, and commands us to love each other. He is disciplined, and gives us the Law of Obedience. He is omniscient, and instructs us to seek knowledge. He works tirelessly in our behalf, and provides us with the Law of Sacrifice. Our covenants with the Lord allow us to grow in wisdom and stature, by providing the cognitive capacity to create a conjoined connection or correlation with the power of conception. It is our covenants that personify or give a face to our Father in Heaven. They fashion an effectual bridge between heaven and earth that allows us to leave the telestial world behind us. Covenants secure our safety as our journey brings us ever closer to celestial realms.

March 7

The
Holy One
(Isaiah 43:15)

The wicked who
delight in iniquity carry a great
burden on their shoulders as they
labor in the darkness, because their level
of understanding and behavior harmonize
with the lowest possible common denominator
of the values and ethics that are embraced by
the world. They do not have the luxury of
knowing **The Holy One**, Who provides
to the faithful the liberating influence
of the key of the mysteries of the
kingdom, even the key of the
knowledge of God.

March 8

Holy, Harmless and Undefiled, Separate from Sinners, and Made Higher than the Heavens
(Hebrews 7:26)

The Lord is **Holy, Harmless And Undefiled, Separate from Sinners, and Made Higher than the Heavens**. His goodness is sufficient to endow us with the power to calibrate our lives to conform to the laws of the Celestial Kingdom.

March 9

The
Hope of Glory
(Colossians 1:27)

The
work of Him
Who is **The Hope of
Glory** is to galvanize our
desire, concentrate our energy,
and crystalize our resolve, to bring
us back to a heavenly home where
delighted Parents are waiting to
greet us with open arms, in
front of a mansion whose
walkways are paved
with gold.

March 10

Immanuel
(Doctrine & Covenants 128:22)

From the
army of Israel,
trumpets are heard,
as banners are unfurled.
Immanuel! God is with us!
The feet of the wicked seem to
have wings as they flutter to and
fro amidst the conflict, and their
soiled garments are rent in the
riotous clash of contrasting
ideologies.

March 11

Jesus our Lord
(Romans 4:24)

If it is our desire to comprehensively embrace the blessings of the Atonement, we must first deny ourselves, and then go with the demanding flow of discipleship. For every good thing lies within the sphere of influence of the Gospel of **Jesus our Lord**.

March 12

The
Judge of All
(Hebrews 12:23)

We may
be assured that
there is One Who stands
before us Who is **The Judge
of All**, and He is eminently fair.
He has provided us with a carefully
calibrated cosmic yardstick with which
we may calculate and quantify the
quality of our obedience, in
order to make necessary
adjustments as we
make our way
home.

March 13

A Priest Forever after
the Order of Melchizedek
(Psalms 110:4)

The
Lord Jesus
Christ is **A Priest
Forever after the Order of
Melchizedek**, and His authority
is the only legitimate power that
has an intrinsic right to rule,
and when the time comes
that His will is done on
earth as it is done in
heaven, all other
powers will
vanish.

March 14

**(He who was) Tempted
in all Points like as we Are**
(Hebrews 4:15)

Too many are
distracted by doctrines
that are not only deceitful,
but that have also been deviously
designed by the devil to destroy our
defenses, deflect our discipleship, dilute
our diligence, discourage our duty, deter
our dedication, and defer our devotion.
How comforting it is to know that He
Who led a perfect and sinless life
was **Tempted in all Points
like as we Are**.

March 15

The Wisdom, Righteousness, Sanctification, and Redemption unto Us
(1 Corinthians 1:30)

We put our
lives and our fortunes
in the hands of Him Who has
provided **Wisdom, Righteousness, Sanctification, and Redemption unto Us**, and willingly pay the asking price, because we know that it is precisely the sum required for the shaping of correct principles.

March 16

My Light and my Salvation
(Psalms 27:1)

"I had rather be a doorkeeper in the house of my God," Who is **My Light and my Salvation**, "than to dwell in the tents of wickedness."
(Psalms 84:10).

March 17

JAH
(Psalms 68:3)

There
are times when
we should not attempt
to bridge with words the gulf
that exists between the secular and
the sacred. It will suffice to lift our voices
unto Jehovah, to "sing praises to his name,
(and to) extol him that rideth upon
the heavens, by his name **JAH**,
(and) rejoice after him."
(Psalms 68:3).

March 18

One God and One Shepherd over All
(1 Nephi 13:41)

Paul taught that there is "One Lord, one faith, one baptism," **One God and One Shepherd over All**.
(Ephesians 4:5).

March 19

Shepherd
(Psalms 23:1)

"Sometimes, we lapse into patterns that seem to stress our accountability for programs rather than for the flock." (Harold B. Lee). While the **Shepherd** is no bean counter, He never gets His priorities confused. He knows each of His sheep by their Christian name.

March 20

He that Liveth
For Ever and Ever
(Revelation 4:9)

To a
spiritually
illiterate world, **He
that Liveth For Ever and Ever**
"gives great lessons in the grammar
of the Gospel." (Neal Maxwell). We learn
from our Divine Tutor that death is simply a
punctuation mark, a comma, a grammatical
device of convenience, that was designed
only to represent the pause between
consecutive breaths. It was never
meant to convey the finality
of an exclamation
mark!

March 21

The Beginning of the Creation of God
(Revelation 3:14)

**The Beginning
of the Creation of God**
established conditions that
allow us to be engaged by our
expedition in mortality, captivated
by its complexity, riveted by
its rewards, immersed in its
intricacies, and wrapped
up in its wonders.

March 22

The Rock of our Redeemer, Who is Christ, the Son of God
(Helaman 5:12)

"Much of what we do organizationally is only scaffolding. As we seek to build individuals, we must not mistake the scaffolding for the soul." (Harold B. Lee). It is people, after all, and not programs, that are the focus of attention of **The Rock of our Redeemer, Who is Christ, the Son of God**.

March 23

He Who Suffered for Us
(1 Peter 2:21)

"We cannot expect a discipleship of unruffled easiness." (Neal A. Maxwell). Fortunately, **He Who Suffered for Us** permits us to burden Him with our cares and concerns, so that we may follow Him without the weight of any regrets, reservations, or restrictions relating to what might have been.

March 24

Meek and Lowly
(Matthew 21:5)

He Who is
Meek and Lowly is
very much like a "bird
that, pausing in her flight
a while on boughs to light,
feels them give way beneath
her, and yet sings, knowing
that she hath wings."
(Victor Hugo).

March 25

The
Savior of Israel
(Acts 13:23)

Jesus Christ,
The Savior of Israel,
works His mighty miracles
through gentle persuasion, because
"force and compulsion will never establish
an ideal society. This can only come through
transformation of the individual soul, and
through a life redeemed from sin and
brought in harmony with divine
will." (David O. McKay).

March 26

Our
Peace
(Ephesians 2:14)

The world
desperately needs
latter-day prophets
who touch our spirits,
precisely because
they speak to
Our Peace.

March 27

The Same Yesterday, Today, and Forever
(Hebrews 13:8)

The Lord creates order and stability out of chaos. He is **The Same Yesterday, Today, and Forever**.

March 28

The Only Begotten of the Father
(John 1:14)

Our undivided and undeviating devotion to **The Only Begotten of the Father** is "the fundamental virtue in religion. If there were more reverence in human hearts, there would be less room for sin and sorrow, and increased capacity for joy and gladness. Reverence for God and sacred things is the chief characteristic of a great soul." (David O. McKay).

March 29

The
Beloved Son
(2 Nephi 31:11)

Happy
are the Saints
who assemble in their
synagogues, enjoying the
companionship of the faithful,
and worshipping **The Beloved Son**.
They shall bear each other up as
on the wings of eagles, as their
assemblies reverberate with
the pleasant sounds of
anticipation.

March 30

Man of Counsel
is My Name
(Moses 7:35)

Man of Counsel is My Name, and I have always revealed to My servants an understanding of their intimate relationship to the timeless nature of celestial realms. To Jeremiah, I explained: "Before I formed thee in the belly I knew thee; and before thou camest forth out of the womb I sanctified thee, and I ordained thee a prophet unto the nations." (Jeremiah 1:4-5).

March 31

The Word of the Lord
(Joshua 22:9)

I will study
the scriptures daily.
In the face of competing
activities, I will persevere.
Though many distractions
vex me incessantly, yet
will I turn my face
to **The Word of
the Lord**.

April 1

The Same Light that Quickeneth your Understanding
(Doctrine & Covenants 88:11)

When the critical hours came in the Garden of Gethsemane, followed by His trial in the court of Pilate, His agony on the Via Dolorosa, and His crucifixion on Calvary, **The Same Light that Quickeneth your Understanding** was able to plumb the limitless depths of Mercy, so much so that Justice itself was satisfied. Having surmounted that formidable hurdle, He could then extend His magnificent forgiveness even to those who had so grievously offended Him.

April 2

The Fear of Isaac
(Genesis 31:42)

Happy are those who plan for the day of adversity. For **The Fear of Isaac** will surely visit the earth with tempests and with famine. Only those who follow the counsel of the prophets will prosper. In the midst of hardship, they will rejoice in their timely preparation.

April 3

He Who was Prepared from the Foundation of the World to Redeem My People
(Ether 3:14)

At the
end of the day,
we rely solely on the
merits of Him **Who was
Prepared from the Foundation
of the World to Redeem** His
People. It is by His grace
alone that we are saved,
after the exhaustion
of all of our own
futile efforts.

April 4

The
Holy Messiah
(2 Nephi 2:6)

The Holy Messiah
asks us to pursue the practice
of prayer a little longer and further.
He knows that when we go the second mile,
we become spiritually independent, and we are
awakened to a greater appreciation of our destiny.
As we study matters out in our own minds preparatory
to receiving answers, we become actively engaged in the
process of inquiry. We dust off our agency, and use it as
it was envisioned. Purposeful prayer allows us to move
beyond the external influences of control, coercion,
intimidation, and compulsion to freedom of
expression and friendly persuasion. We
expand our capabilities as we exercise
the gifts, resources, and reserves
provided by our Father's
perfect Plan of
Salvation.

April 5

The Light and
the Life of the World
(Doctrine & Covenants 34:2)

There
will always be
shadows, especially
when the sun is brightly
shining. But if we keep our
faces oriented toward **The Light
and the Life of the World**,
darkness will always
be behind
us.

April 6

King
of Zion
(Moses 7:53)

Is there a key to
happiness, or an answer to
where we can find the peace
that surpasses understanding?
The simple truth is that it
is in the **King of Zion**
alone that all of our
needs may be
satisfied.

April 7

In all Things
(Doctrine & Covenants 88:41)

Latter-day Saints tend to emphasize the Savior's experience while in the Garden of Gethsemane as the pivotal event leading to His sacrifice, but we can see that it was really a many-faceted drama played out on different stages. It began even before the creation of the earth, for the scriptures identify Jesus Christ as "the Lamb slain from the foundation of the world." (Revelation 13:8). It will only end when the last repentant sinner has received intercession by Him Who is **In All Things**, and has obtained forgiveness by the Father. In the meantime, our injunction is to develop every characteristic of our Savior, and to become as He is. As we internalize His divine attributes, we will become perfected in Him.

April 8

Endless and
Eternal is My Name
(Moses 7:35)

**Endless
and Eternal is
My Name** and my less
disciplined family members
must be perfect in their repentance
before they can return to our heavenly
home. They need to follow My example
as they grow from innocent childhood,
through tumultuous adolescence,
and on to spiritual wisdom
and maturity.

April 9

Chosen of God and Precious
(1 Peter 2:4)

The **Chosen of God and Precious** gives us opportunities for growth that require strength, moral courage, and the ability to prioritize our time, so that we can focus on matters of substance. Every week, each of us has 168 hours, much of it discretionary time. We can do with it as we please. We need to ask ourselves: How are we managing that priceless gift?

April 10

God and the Father
of our Lord Jesus Christ
(Colossians 1:3)

Many years ago, a movie entitled "Heaven Can Wait" was released, that told the story of a man who cheated death, in a way, and was allowed a second chance to live his life. As I thought about the film, it struck me that today **God and the Father of our Lord Jesus Christ** has blessed me to be able to enjoy a milestone in my own life. I've lived one day longer than ever before, and in doing so have set a new personal record for longevity. At least for now, or so it seems, heaven can wait! Today I have been given another chance to get it right.

April 11

The Blood of Jesus Christ Cleanseth us from all Sin
(1 John 1:7)

The introduction of the concept of opposition into the peaceful environment enjoyed by Adam and Eve in the Garden negated their naivety, pummeled their purity, and violated their virtue. The scriptures attest to the telestial turmoil that resulted from the disruption of their idyllic existence. But these same scriptures describe a transformation from a morally static environment to one infused with the promise of progression through the exercise of free will. When their eyes had been opened, our first parents were taught that **The Blood of Jesus Christ Cleanseth us from all Sin**.

April 12

By Whom God Made the Worlds
(Hebrews 1:2)

We owe
not only our devotion
but also our active support,
to Him **By Whom God Made the Worlds**. We cannot avoid our duty any more than could Jonah. Were we to attempt to do so, we would be swallowed up by a leviathan no less real, and eventually spit out on the rocky shoreline of our obligations.

April 13

God the Father and the
Lord Jesus Christ our Saviour
(Titus 1:4)

The
riveting atmosphere
in heaven surrounding the
events that transpired at the
Council of **God the Father and
the Lord Jesus Christ our Saviour**
underscores our need to work within
celestially inspired guidelines to achieve
spiritual resolutions related to the execution
of the rules and regulations that govern the
world in which we live. Our meaningful
participation in the process by which
order in society is maintained,
without the prostitution of
our core principles, can
be challenging, but
is necessary.

April 14

(He) Hath an Unchangeable Priesthood
(Hebrews 7:24)

The concept of covenants goes back to Abraham and beyond, and concerns agreements that are made with God, Who **Hath an Unchangeable Priesthood**. In recognition of the righteousness of the Father of the Faithful, the Lord made promises to him and to his descendants. The Abrahamic Covenant, as these pledges are called, is of such power and scope that its conditions bless all of Heavenly Father's children with the opportunity to participate in the Plan of Salvation and receive the rights, privileges, and responsibilities relating to eternal progression.

April 15

(He) Hath Given us Understanding that we may Know Him that is True
(1 John 5:20)

Inasmuch as
knowledge is related to the
righteous application of power,
God **Hath Given us Understanding
that we may Know Him that is True**. As
their comprehension of the principles of the
Plan expands, members of His Church are given
the opportunity to make a number of promises to the
Author of our salvation. There are baptismal, sacramental,
and temple covenants, as well as the Oath and Covenant of
the Priesthood. If God did not make binding contracts
with His children, if there were no law given, if we
could sin with impunity, "what could justice do,
or mercy either, for they would have no claim
upon the creature? The works of justice
would be destroyed, and God
would cease to be God."
(Alma 42:21-22).

April 16

Eternal Redemption for Us
(Hebrews 9:12)

Lehi taught
that in order for us to grow,
our mortal experience requires that
we face opposition. But this fundamental
principle of the Plan of Salvation does not give
us license to act recklessly, or to capitulate to the Dark
Side the minute our belief systems have been challenged.
He Whose sacrifice promises **Eternal Redemption for Us**
tolerates, and in a sense may even embrace, opposition,
because He knows we have the innate capacity to
develop the moral backbone to meet prejudice
with impartiality, narrow-mindedness with
limitless opportunity for expression,
unforgiveness with compassion,
and disrespect with
consideration.

April 17

He is Above all Things, and is Through all Things, and is Round about all Things
(Doctrine & Covenants 88:41)

He
Who **is**
Above all Things
and is Through all Things,
and is Round about all Things
may be contrasted with the unilaterally
dogmatic posturing of Lucifer, who would
have had us believe that his counterfeit proposal
could have granted admonishment without adaptation,
absolution without apology, rebuke without resolution,
rectification without reinforcement, amelioration without
acquittal, alteration without affection, reproach without
reassurance, correction without concern, pacification
without propitiation, chastisement without charity,
reproof without reconciliation, amendment
without admiration, and indebtedness
without indemnification.

April 18

El-elohe-Israel
(Genesis 33:20)

El-elohe-Israel,
otherwise known as the
mighty God of Israel, guides
and blesses us, with the qualifying
modifier thrown in that we have agency.
At first glance, control and free will appear to
be antithetical, but they are actually in harmony if
we think of them as dynamic counterparts that are the
fundamental elements of a volatile process that leads us
to an expansive and unrestrained reality called eternal life
that can only be fully appreciated when it is contrasted with
spiritual death. We realize that control on the one hand,
and the freedom to act independently on the other,
are the yin and yang of the opposition in all
things that was described by Lehi, and
that "if these things are not,"
then "there is no God."
(2 Nephi 2:13).

April 19

In the Beginning, Before the World Was
(Doctrine & Covenants 93:7)

Soon after the
expulsion of Adam and
Eve from the Garden, agitators
for social change probed the limits of
their newfound independence, in contrast to
their parents' lifestyle of moderation and restraint.
One thing became almost immediately apparent. The
image and likeness of God that had been so familiar in
the Garden was unrecognizable in the urban jungle east
of Eden. In tattoo parlors and crystal palaces, the sons
and daughters of Adam and Eve festooned their
bodies and pierced their skin with the logos of
lasciviousness. They unconsciously defined
themselves by a caricature of a previously
cherished purity. Telestial trappings
disrupted their awareness of the
Lord, Whose presence had
been **In the Beginning,
before the World
Was**.

April 20

The Lord
is Among Us
(Joshua 22:31)

To put a positive
spin on things, we mortals
have become perfect runway models,
warts and all, to showcase opposition. We
have all witnessed those who have vacationed
in Idumea to celebrate the festival of free will and
the carnival of carefree living. But we also remember
Paul, who shed telestial trappings to experience a
more profound comprehension of reality. His
example teaches us that **The Lord is Among
Us**, and that "now" and "eternity" are but
distinctive manifestations of the same
seamless reality, and are only
distinguished by very
subtle shades of
difference.

April 21

The
Just Lord
(Zephaniah 3:5)

Agency is
the lynchpin of the
Plan of Happiness, and **The
Just Lord** uses its principles to provide
us with the means to take upon ourselves His
armour, our loins girt about with truth and with the
breastplate of righteousness, and our feet shod with the
preparation of the gospel of peace. We don the helmet
of salvation, and grasp the sword of the Spirit. Over
time, these noble qualities are amalgamated into an
impenetrable shield of faith that facilitates our
stability as we negotiate uneven terrain on
our journey through mortality. We are
unencumbered by the inappropriate
or misguided trappings of control
and restraint that would only
impede our progress.

April 22

He Who Came unto His Own
(Doctrine & Covenants 88:48)

He Who Came unto His Own has provided
an Atonement that extends to us
the invitation both to forgive and to
be forgiven, in sharp contrast to the sense
of despair, despondency, misery, and
hopelessness that would have been
ours had we been left without
a Redeemer, to deal with
our failures, as well as
the shortcomings
of others,
alone.

April 23

Him that is True
(1 John 5:20)

The Savior is **Him that is True**, and He asks us to journey along a difficult path that may lead to the court of Pilate, there to experience false accusations at the hands of others. It is necessary for us to lead Christ-like lives, even if that means we must experience a scourging from those who seek to do us harm.

April 24

I am the
Lord thy God
(2 Nephi 8:16)

With Einstein's redefinition of the equations of time, the only temporal dimension with which we have experience has revealed a mercurial side to its nature. It is now common to use the expression: "It's all relative." The assurance of Jesus Christ: **I am the Lord thy God**, speaks to His permanence, but it also allows us to enjoy the passage of time at our own unhurried pace, while still maintaining unshaken confidence in His omnisicence, His omnipotence, and His omnipresence.

April 25

I am the True Light
that is in You
(Doctrine & Covenants 88:50)

Our normal lifespan
gives us ample opportunity
to develop patience as we bide our
time, mature in discipline as we take time,
delight in diligence as we make time, expand our
care and concern as we find time, cultivate wisdom as
we invest time, enhance our thoughtfulness as we spend
time, and experience pleasure as we share time. The tempo
of life becomes a useful school master when we use it to
bask in the warm embrace of our Savior, and
engage the curriculum of the One Who
assures us: **I am the True Light
that is in You.**

April 26

I am the
Father and the Son
(Ether 3:14)

The latter-
day restoration
of the Gospel has been a
process of evolution. It wasn't
until April 26, 1838, for example,
that **the Father and the Son** revealed:
"For thus shall my church be called in the
last days, even the Church of Jesus Christ of
Latter-day Saints." (D&C 115:4). Beforehand, the
Church had been variously called the Church
of Christ, the Church of Jesus Christ, the
Church of God, and the Church of the
Latter-day Saints. Even today, it is
sometimes erroneously called
the Mormon Church, or the
L.D.S. Church.

April 27

God our Father
and Jesus Christ our Lord
(2 Timothy 1:2)

During the centuries after the mortal ministry of the Savior, there was gradual but accelerating apostasy from the truth, culminating in a doctrinal free-fall that shattered any resemblance of the Church to its original features. The Dark Ages inevitably followed. Clearly, **God our Father and Jesus Christ our Lord** would need to restore the authority of the priesthood so that the glory days of Their One True Church might be reestablished on the earth.

April 28

He that Giveth Salvation unto Kings
(Psalms 144:10)

The Gospel is the New and Everlasting Covenant. It has been ordained by His everlasting authority and will never be changed or abandoned. Throughout history, **He that Giveth Salvation unto Kings** has enjoyed a covenant relationship with His Chosen People. Each time the Gospel is restored after being taken from the earth as a result of apostasy, it is new to those who receive it.

April 29

In Whom is Salvation
(2 Timothy 2:10)

In the adventure film "Indiana Jones and The Last Crusade," the Grail Knight tells Indie: "You must choose. But choose wisely, for as the true Grail will bring you life, the false Grail will take it from you." The Gospel Plan that has received the endorsement of the Lord, **In Whom is Salvation**, teaches us how to choose wisely. We need to do it, do it right, and do it right now, because "there's no time like the present, no present like time, and life can be over in the space of a rhyme."
(Georgia Byng).

April 30

Left us
an Example
(1 Peter 2:21)

Opposition can
be a positive motivator
when it allows us to gauge the
success of our internalization of the
Plan's provisions, and when it gives us
a sense of how we are doing in our efforts
to energetically participate without deviation in
purposeful programs of personal progress propelling
us forward on proven paths of propriety leading to
unparalleld prosperity. Our conformity to the
perfect pattern of the Savior, Who **Left us
an Example**, has the capacity to provide
significant sustainable support, as we
feel the innate upward reach of the
Plan and are carried aloft, as
upon the wings of eagles,
by its principles.

May 1

The
Light of Christ
(Doctrine & Covenants 88:7)

It is within the
warm embrace of **The
Light of Christ** that we are led
to an appreciation that our Father in
Heaven has established His covenant to
release us from our bondage to sin. It sets
us free to take advantage of every feature of
the Plan of Salvation. Without redemption,
that is integral to the covenant, we realize
that the purpose of the Plan would have
been frustrated. Because of the Savior's
Atonement, however, we may escape
the icy fingers of the death-grip of
Satan, who is patiently waiting
to drag our willing souls
down to the depths
of hell.

May 2

The Light which Shineth, which Giveth you Light
(Doctrine & Covenants 88:11)

Where is everybody?
Are we alone in the universe?
If you lift your eyes and strain to see
beyond your limited horizons, **The Light which Shineth, which Giveth you Light**, will provide the answer, and you will find yourself cast off into a stream of expanding self-awareness and carried along in quickening currents that will take you on a fantastic journey to a far country. You might even come to the point where you begin to appreciate that "the universe is a machine for the making of gods." (Henri Bergson). As Q told Captain Picard: "Con permiso, Capitán. The hall is rented, the orchestra engaged. It's now time to see if you can dance." ("Q Who?").

May 3

Lord God of Abraham,
Isaac, and of Israel
(1 Chronicles 29:18)

In our
fallen state, we are
the enemies of the **Lord
God of Abraham, Isaac, and
of Israel**, and have been from the
beginning. Our behavior that involves
the inappropriate exercise of our agency,
as well as manifestations of inequality and
disparity, may simply represent the natural
consequences of imbalance in our lives.
If so, its effects will be inevitable and
inexorable unless the Author of
Salvation and the Maker and
Fashioner of the universe
intervenes through the
utilization of higher
laws that trump
disproportion.

May 4

**Lord God of
Israel our Father**
(1 Chronicles 29:10)

The catalyzing
influence of agency
brings time and space
into perfect harmony and
allows us to reassess, regroup,
repent, and recommit. Under the
nurturing influence of the **Lord God
of Israel our Father**, these three elements
have been designed to combine into a single
clarifying creation that can coalesce within the
crucible of experience into a comprehension
of capacity that can no longer condone
complacency but rather commands
commitment to a constructive
conclusion to every
challenge.

May 5

The Name of the Lord
(Genesis 4:26)

We are the players in an interstellar balancing act that extends all the way to the end of the cosmos. It harmonizes the exercise of moral agency with the implementation in our behalf of other equally important and co-existing laws, all in **The Name of the Lord** who rules on earth and in the heavens. Mercy, in particular, exists to mitigate the otherwise inevitable consequences related to disproportion when lives are out of balance. The gyroscopic nature of the Atonement stabilizes our foundation and re-establishes a sense of equilibrium even in our small corner of His vineyard.

May 6

His Arrow Shall go forth as the Lightning
(Zechariah 9:14)

Surely, we must be living in heaven right now. I feel your pain and loss, as well as your pleasure and gain. Heaven cannot wait, because **His Arrow Shall go forth as the Lightning**. To facilitate our desire to perfom acts of Quiet Christianity, God has abundantly blessed us with the capacity for consideration, concern, compassion, kindness, understanding and empathy. Benign benevolence is blind to hypocrisy, and helps us to relate to messages that resonate with truth, such as: "Never send to know for whom the bell tolls; it tolls for thee. " (John Donne).

May 7

Made of a Woman
(Galatians 4:4)

After the Fall,
Satan exulted in his
new role as the de-facto
god of this earth, replacing
Him Who would be **Made of a Woman**. He believed that he had
thwarted the Plan by metaphorically
bringing to the attention of Adam and Eve
their nakedness. More literally, his nefarious
scheme was designed to expose their vulnerability
by penetrating their celestial skin and causing its
contamination with the worldly elements of
transgression. The tempter fancied himself
a telestial tailor who could somehow
legitimize, or at least secularize,
the indiscretion of Adam
and Eve by hiding their
nakedness from
God.

May 8

Made Under the Law
(Galatians 4:4)

In a sense, we become new creatures in Christ because we maintain perfect symmetry, oriented more to the laws of the eternal world and to the guidance of the Master Who was **Made Under the Law**, than to the limitations imposed by the physical world and the destructive effects of disproportion. Whosoever is born of God overcomes the laws governing our mortal sojourn. This transformative experience is inexplicable, and yet it is undeniable. It is a process of generation, and not only of maturation.

May 9

My Strength, and my Fortress, and my Refuge in the Day of Affliction
(Jeremiah 16:19)

The adversary is
flushed with excitement,
because he knows how difficult it is
for me to resist my natural tendency toward
volatility. But God is **My Strength, and my Fortress,
and my Refuge in the Day of Affliction,** and I know that,
even though my inattention to celestial sign-posts leads me
onto crooked paths of self-destructive and self-defeating
behaviors, and an unbalanced life points me toward
inevitable and ultimate destruction, I can always
rely upon the intervention of higher laws that
will allow me to get back onto the strait
and narrow path, after having paid
the appropriate fine. At least I
know that the premium is
fixed on my eternal life
insurance policy.

May 10

(He) of Whom are all Things
(1 Corinthians 8:6)

Our natural element is heaven, and its aether fills our lungs with celestial air. It is the state of being to which we all intuitively aspire. When He **of Whom are all Things** created the earth, He established laws to govern it that were designed to facilitate our journey Home. We are spiritual beings having mortal experiences, and sometimes feel that we are out synch and do not belong here. If that is so, our true greatness, and our power, will only be manifest when "the stars fade away, the sun himself grow dim with age, and nature sink in years." Then, we "shall flourish in immortal youth, unhurt amidst the war of elements, the wreck of matter, and the crash of worlds." (Joseph Addision).

May 11

One
Body
(1 Corinthians 12:12)

As we abide celestial law, the
Spirit will open our eyes, "so as to
see and understand the things of God,"
Who is **One Body**, "even those things which
were from the beginning before the world was."
(D&C 76:12-13). We will comprehend even more clearly
when we have escaped the confining limitations of our
mortal clay that so persistently drag our attention
to the upsetting and destabilizing character
flaws of carnality and sensuality, and to
an uneven nature that denies the
power of the Atonement.

May 12

Our Life
(Colossians 3:4)

When we
find out where we
came from, why we are here,
and where we are going, the powers
of creation are unleashed in our behalf and we
experience the exhilaration of a personally tailored "Big
Bang" moment. **Our Life** takes on new dimensions. It is as if
we are present at the moment of creation itself. Our power
"to become" is released from the oppressive bondage of
ignorance and from self-defeating behaviors spawned
by arrogance. The genesis of the universe falls into
a comprehensible perspective and creates a
context and continuity that allows our
perception of reality to align with
eternal principles and expand
to proportions that are
mind-boggling.

May 13

Potter
(Isaiah 64:8)

Progress is
the recompense for
perseverance, salvation is the
reward for surmounting obstacles,
and the hope of eternal life is the blessing
for enduring opposition. By delicately balancing
our experiences, we become more comfortable with
the realization that confirms that Gospel principles
relating to the eternities might supersede physical
laws that pertain only to the temporal universe.
When we engage the **Potter** in His studio, and
we begin to turn on His wheel, it is the
covenants we make with Him that
mold and shape us into a form
that permits us to ascend to
dizzying heights without
experiencing vertigo.
We are Born
Again.

May 14

The
Prophet
(John 7:40)

If we are
not careful, and we
nurture a one-dimensional
view of the world that focuses on
its cares, or if we yield to the trivialities
that so persistently demand our undivided
attention, or if we lose our balance and then trip
over ourselves in a feverish pursuit of the flavor of
the day, we will inevitably fall into mischief. **The
Prophet** is able to help us to develop poise under
pressure if we allow Him to provide us with the
multidimensional view of our existence that
creates an accurate and realistic context in
which to wisely exercise our agency.
Our comprehension may intitally
take our breath away, but our
lungs will soon fill anew
with celestial
air.

May 15

Rock of Offense
(1 Peter 2:8)

If we stumble at the manner and place of the birth of Jesus, at His parentage, and at his education and trade as a carpenter, at His poverty and at the obscurity of His kingdom, at His doctrine and His miracles, at the audiences who attended Him, and at the company He kept, and even at the manner of His betrayal, His death, and His crucifixion, He will be a **Rock of Offense**.

May 16

Our
Savior
(1 Timothy 2:3)

Our Savior is
the Author of the greatest
diversity on our planet. He invented it
when He divided the light from the darkness,
the waters from the firmament, the heaven from the
earth, the land from the sea, the day from the night, and
when He formed all manner of living things, each to go forth
and multiply after its own kind. His penultimate act of
creative diversity was when He made men and
women. For all we know, He may have
even fashioned Mars and Venus as
their respective habitations.

May 17

Separate from Sinners
(Hebrews 7:26)

Since most of us have not yet completed enough of the curriculum of the Gospel to master the skills necessary to be the successful architects of our own fate, we are commanded: "Give your language to exhortation continually." (D&C 23:7). The Savior would keep us **Separate from Sinners**, from those who go to great lengths to throw us off balance. Those who are Born Again require the constant and repetitive encouragement of positive peer pressure to strengthen their resolve, steady their course, and continue the process of their progression. As Paul exhorted us: "Let us not weary in well doing."
(Galatians 6:9).

May 18

Thou, Whose name alone is Jehovah,
art the Most High over all the Earth
(Psalms 83:18)

Satan, who was a liar
from the beginning, believed that
by violating the sanctity of the Garden and
deceiving Eve, he would be able to irreparably
compromise the spiritual fortification that had been
provided by Heavenly Father. During the anticipated
confusion after the Fall, it was his devious design to install
himself as a puppet ruler, a demagogue, a political agitator,
a crowd-pleaser, and become the god of this world. What he
had not counted on, however, was the fact that it was their
divine nature that had provided our first parents with
protection from his evil influence. All that would be
necessary to restore their purity and the stability
that they had enjoyed in Eden, was the further
light and knowledge that they had been
promised by God, **Whose name alone
is Jehovah**, Who is **the Most High
over all the Earth**. The devil
never saw that one
coming.

May 19

Shall Appear the Second Time without Sin unto Salation
(Hebrews 9:23)

Satan
believed that by
partaking of the forbidden
fruit, the natural defense systems
of Adam and Eve had been irreversibly
weakened. But the Lord, who sees the end
from the beginning, and Who **Shall Appear the
Second Time without Sin unto Salvation**, countered
by promising them further light and knowledge even
after their expulsion from Eden. This pattern
provided a means for the redemption of
not only Adam and Eve, but also
of their posterity.

May 20

Stone
of Stumbling
(1 Peter 2:8)

If we
wish to
approach the
character of Jesus,
we must internalize the
quality of charity. The two
go hand in hand and to presume
one without the other is unthinkable.
Charity is the pure love of Christ and
it need not be articulated, for it is by
our works that we shall be known.
To do good for any reason other
than for the glory of God is to
view the Lord as a **Stone of
Stumbling** that will put
us in jeopardy of
condemnation.

May 21

**The Light which is in all Things,
which Giveth Life to all Things**
(Doctrine & Covenants 88:13)

God's pattern
provides opportunities
for us to put our fingers on our
pulse to test the promises of His Plan's
guiding principles. He is the quintessential
travel agent, Who has arranged interesting side
trips and excursions for us to take during our journey.
These have been designed to expand our appreciation of
life's real purpose, which is to have learning experiences
through interaction with the wonders of the world. To
accomplish this, we must adopt the itinerary of **The
Light which is in all Things, which Giveth
Life to all Things**. All we need to take
with us to satisfy our needs, is
the currency of faith.

May 22

Elohim
(Bible Dictionary, p. 661)

As we
prostrate ourselves
before the face of **Elohim**,
we grow weak in His Presence.
He is almighty, omnipotent, and is
incomprehensible. The pleasing bar of
Christ is continually before us, as we
prepare ever so inadequately; and
yet we grow in His grace, that
we may confidently awaken
to greet each dawn as a
brighter day.

May 23

Thy Name
is from Everlasting
(Isaiah 63:16)

Isaiah
recognized
Jehovah as the
Lamb Who had been
slain from the foundation
of the world, and exclaimed:
Thy Name is from Everlasting!
Long before he uttered these revealing
words, the Savior had begun to consistently
accumulate reserves in His own spiritual
bank account against the day when He
would need them the most. He knew
from the beginning, even before
the Plan had been explained
to His Father's children,
that His Atonement
would be both
infinite and
eternal.

May 24

True Light
(1 John 2:8)

In our
friends, we look for
the traits of unselfishness,
honesty, integrity, kindness, and
charity. They would never think to
contribute to our delinquency, misery,
or hardship. Instead, they leave us better
than when they found us. We should
all strive to be more like the **True
Light**, to be the kinds of people
our dogs think we are.

May 25

The
True Vine
(John 15:1)

We prosper from
the Plan of Salvation when we
pay close attention to its priorities.
Proper prior parental planning prevents
poor priesthood performance. To that end,
in our pre-earth existence, a Council was held
to pre-emptively obtain our informed consent
and endorsement of the principles of the Plan,
prior to our departure for earth. During that
symposium, God outlined His vision for our
continuing progression, but also entertained
alternative proposals. He then moderated a
discussion of the risks that would be taken
by those who would choose to participate
in His ordained program. He answered
questions, anticipating the interjections
of those who would be quick to foster
a rebellion. Everything we are can
be traced back to **The True Vine**
Who was then, and is now,
our only Source.

May 26

The Voice of One Crying in the Wilderness
(Doctrine & Covenants 88:66)

The journey
from our first estate
through the birth canal into
the expanse of the wide, wide world
was breathtaking. The memory of our
former life was erased, but new vistas soon
opened up to fill in the void. To reinforce our
understanding of the principles we had aforetime
internalized, religious recognition, a re-cognition, a
re-knowing, or an intuitive remembrance of our
former glory, came into play. **The Voice of
One Crying in the Wilderness** would
ring a familiar bell and stir our
memories. To describe the
process, the expression
"deja-vu" was
coined.

May 27

Who Shall Judge the Quick and the Dead
(2 Timothy 4:1)

The Atonement of Him **Who Shall Judge the Quick and the Dead** took into account every sin that would be committed by the children of God from the foundation of the world. It anticipated the shortcomings that would be repetitively, painfully, and frustratingly exhibited by every generation from the beginning to the end of time. It is all the more remarkable that the Atonement was able to foresee our sins that had not yet been committed. The price necessary to satisfy Justice and obtain Mercy was paid well in advance, and thankfully, the accounting process was completed without slapping on interest, late fees, or service charges. Our credit score can remain a perfect 850.

May 28

Who
Knew no Sin
(2 Corinthians 5:21)

The crucified Christ
is the primary focus of
Christianity, but if we fail to
understand Him **Who Knew no
Sin** during His mortal ministry, we
risk receiving only a one-dimensional
view that ignores the wonderful harmony
between His humanity and His divinity. When
we have known personal hardship ourselves
and develop empathy, we learn to overlook
the shortcomings of others and to forgive
them their trespasses. As we become
less judgmental, they are more
likely to turn to us for help
in dealing with their
own challenges.

May 29

Who is Passed into the Heavens
(Hebrews 4:14)

Sometimes,
it is difficult to be
happy about the success of
others. We believe that if someone
else is recognized for their achievement,
it will diminish us. Your "A" will overshadow
my "B." Your church calling is more significant than
mine. Your mission assignment is more glamourous than
mine. You seem to have many talents, and I have so few.
You're a stud-muffin and I'm such a geek. Your car
is way cooler than my beater. Your degree, your
education, your house, your kids, and your
vacations. It will never, ever end, if we
allow our focus to wander from Him
Who is Passed into the Heavens.

May 30

Your Father, and your God, and my God
(Doctrine & Covenants 88:75)

Pride and petty jealousy are seductively effective satanic tools designed to negatively impact our spiritual well-being. "When pride has a hold on our hearts, we lose our independence and deliver our freedoms to the bondage of men's judgment." (Ezra Taft Benson). In a shouting contest, the world will always prevail if we ignore the quiet counsel of **Your Father, and your God, and my God**.

May 31

Voice of Thunderings
(Doctrine & Covenants 88:90)

If the mighty **Voice of Thunderings** does not speak today, perhaps it is because He cannot. Perhaps He has suffered a massive stroke resulting in aphasia. Maybe He has lost His First Amendment rights, and no longer enjoys freedom of speech. Maybe He has developed xenophobia. Maybe He has retreated behind the walls of His kingdom because He feels intimidated by those who insist that He does not exist. Maybe He just doesn't care about His children anymore. His silence might be evidence that He has lost interest in us, has other things on His mind, has other priorities, or has become distracted by more pressing concerns.
Probably not.

June 1

The Voice of Lightnings
(Doctrine & Covenants 88:90)

Could
it be that **The
Voice of Lightnings**
is daunted by our advances
in the healing arts and feels that
His nurturing powers have become
obsolete? Maybe the information technology
explosion has intimidated Him. Maybe He feels
overshadowed by our advances in education; that
Common Core has leveled the playing field so that the
need for pointed and specific religious instruction no
longer exists. Maybe He has grown weary of the
avalanche of negative press in media that has
its own agenda. Maybe He has nothing to
add to the dialogue, because we have
things figured out on our own, and
are securely in control of our
own destiny. Maybe,
or maybe not.

June 2

The Voice of Tempests
(Doctrine & Covenants 88:90)

The Voice of Tempests
can speak to His children however
and whenever He wishes. The scriptures
reveal how deeply He has always cared about
us, how intensely He has been interested in our
welfare, and how intertwined are our lives with His
work and glory. It seems clear that He would no
more abandon us to our own devices, than we
would leave a toddler unattended in a dark
alleyway in the bad part of town. He
would never forsake us or
require us to fend for
ourselves.

June 3

The Voice of the Waves of the Sea Heaving Themselves Beyond their Bounds.
(Doctrine & Covenants 88:90)

Surely,
we need wise
counsel now as much as
we ever have, because we have
the potential to destroy each other
and our world if we do not follow **The
Voice of the Waves of the Sea Heaving
Themselves Beyond their Bounds**. We need
Him and His living prophets today, as did the
Saints in times of old, to provide triage when
dealing with telestial trauma. We need to
be shown how to negotiate mortality's
minefields, help to free ourselves
from conceptual quicksands,
and inspired gudance to
deal with doctrinal
dead ends.

June 4

My Son
(Psalms 2:7)

Genetic diversity
within a population promotes
robust and resilient organisms that more
vigorously resist disease. This may be one reason
why converts often become the strength of the Church.
They introduce new chromosomal material that expands
the genome of the members and gives it elasticity. Then,
when our collective testimonies have been nourished by
rich Gospel soil, their shoots will be protected from the
withering sun in the heat of the day. In the Church, the
whole is greater than the sum of its parts. Although
we may be Israelites by adoption, and have come
to Zion from the four corners of the earth, we
realize that there is within each of us a
common autobiographical thread
leading all the way back to
heaven, to Him Who
was called **My
Son**.

June 5

Through all Things
(Doctrine & Covenants 88:41)

The Savior of the
world, Who has been
Through all Things, has a
knack for seeing the principle of
agency in a different light. He realizes
that the exercise of free will entails risk, that
the element of failure is real and is always just
one decision away, but He knows that experience
is the only way to lay claim to unspeakable joy in our
Father's kingdom. He gives us repetitive opportunities
to recommit ourselves to our covenants, and teaches
us that the laws pertaining to happiness are tied
to obedience. With encouraging words, He
continually nurtures our spiritual well-
being, inner peace, harmony,
and cheerfulness.

June 6

Round About all Things
(Doctrine & Covenants 88:41)

Our
living prophet
not only shares our
perspective, but he also
sees through the clarifying
and purifying lens of eternity.
He can see **Round About all Things**.
Our lives are blessed in many ways by
his nurturing influence that comes from
a profound understanding of the Plan
of Salvation. The veil that has been
drawn over our eyes, preventing
us from seeing our potential
with an unimpeded view,
is, for him, nearly
transparent.

June 7

The Confidence of all the Ends of the Earth
(Psalms 65:5)

Perhaps one of the greatest contributions of **The Confidence of all the Ends of the Earth** was His teaching about what is in store for each of us. How He conducted His life, endured His suffering, dignified His death, and celebrated His Resurrection, clarifies our understanding of heaven and makes it seem real. By precept and example, He has shown us the way.

June 8

A Shepherd in the Land
(Zechariah 11:16)

There is
A Shepherd in the Land Who can provide
protection from both ravenous wolves
who harass the flock, and from our own foibles
that more insidiously destabilize our spirituality. He
has within His arsenal enough firepower to provide
the means for us to overcome unsteadiness in our
lives, and then, unencumbered by wobbly
constraints, to move onward and
upward along a steady
course of eternal
progress.

June 9

Horn of David
(Psalms 132:17)

The Horn of David has promised the Saints that when Zion is tried and tested in the fiery crucible of mortal experience, personal righteousness will be her fortress and her sanctuary. To the world, she is a living testament of the potential for goodness that can be found in all mankind. She stands as an example that the reward of faith is celestial surety.

June 10

Another Comforter
(John 14:6)

Redundancy
has been built into the
Plan of Salvation. It provides
for **Another Comforter**, Whose
companionship has created an added
layer of protection and a second source of
inspiration, as we encounter opposition during
our journey through mortality. If we "defriend"
the Savior and turn our backs on Him, we deny
ourselves the opportunity we might have had
to enjoy a very special relationship that could
have matured into a fantastic odyssey with
an ever-faithful traveling companion. He
could have ultimately accompanied us
to a far country, where we might
have been introduced by His
Father to the Celestial
Kingdom.

June 11

A Light that is Endless
(Mosiah 16:9)

What are we to do?
How can we find the truth?
To whom can we turn for guidance
and direction? Have the heavens closed?
Are they silent? Are we to be left alone, to
wander to and fro, like flotsam on the sea of
life? Does God answer our prayers? Has
revelation ceased? Will we live again?
The questions go on forever, but
the answers are simple, for
the Lord is **A Light
that is Endless**.

June 12

El
(Bible Dictionary, p. 661)

In our society,
we frequently believe that
retribution is our right and our
responsibility. Too many religions
exercise a sword of vengeance as their
God-given duty. The example of **El**
teaches lessons about forgiveness,
as well as about unconditional
love and selfless sacrifice,
that fly in the face of
conventional
wisdom.

June 13

King
of Israel
(Matthew 27:42)

We
may feel
that we are the
architects of our own
fate, and that our agency
correctly applied will see the
building fitly framed. But beyond
our own puny efforts, there is a greater
power at work. **The King of Israel** is
able to stay well within budget
guidelines and still transform
our poor habitations into
royal mansions.

June 14

The
Lord of Sabaoth
(Doctrine & Covenants 95:7)

Balance
is at the very heart
of the eternal laws that are
employed by **The Lord of Sabaoth**.
These laws have the capacity to carry us
beyond the conventional boundaries of our
everyday world. Our five natural senses enable
us to relate to our physical surroundings. They act as
barometers that provide us with reliable measurements
to gauge the inexorable effects of imbalance that almost
imperceptibly wear us down. When we are "born
of God," however, we are oriented more to the
expansive laws of the eternal world than
we are to restrictive temporal contracts.
When we are in harmony with the
eternities, we are in a better
state of balance.

June 15

The
Lord Omnipotent
(Mosiah 3:5)

Our
doubts obscure
the true vision of the
heart, while belief in **The
Lord Omnipotent** leads us
to undeniable testimony
and replaces fear with
saving faith.

June 16

The
Lord's Christ
(Luke 2:26)

The
earth is
the footstool of
The Lord's Christ.
We leave to His better
judgment the bestowal of its
treasures, and turn our attention
instead, to the unfathomable riches of
eternity. Too often, though, mammon
can be the focus of our thoughts. It
clutches us in its strong grip, and
captures our attention in a fierce
competition with our better
nature, leaving soul scars
and indelible stains on
our character that
only repentance
can remove.

June 17

My Light and my Salvation
(Psalms 27:1)

Imbalance in the
temporal world that leads me
from order to disorder suits the purposes of
Him Who is **My Light and my Salvation**, as long
as the created confusion jars me out of my collective
complacency. If imbalance upsets the status quo,
makes me think, gets my juices flowing, prods
me to purposefully expend my energy,
and constructively puts my agency
to work, it will have served
a useful purpose.

June 18

The Son of Abraham
(Matthew 1:1)

When the Holy Ghost sheds light on the weightier matters of the law, we are infused with a liberating sense of independence, as we absorb someting new every day. A breathtaking expansion of understanding illuminates our hearts and our minds. When our learning style embraces the Spirit, we discover a pattern that becomes our norm. Our comprehension of true principles is built upon our absorption of light and knowledge, until we arrive at a point where our testimonies of the divinity of **The Son of Abraham** are independent and unshakable. Our witnesses stand on the solid foundation of faith and require no external warrant.

June 19

The Lord
God of Israel
(Luke 1:68)

**The Lord
God of Israel** helps
us to forget our bad days
and to focus on becoming better; to
love our families; to be more responsible
towards others, and to help them; to sacrifice
ourselves through His love; to try to create a
little bit of heaven on earth; to make a
small contribution to the welfare of
our neighbors, and to assist
others on their journey
to Christ.

June 20

The Lord is Able to Deliver Us
(1 Nephi 4:3)

God is
our Father, and
He is perfect in every
way. He is **Able to Deliver Us**.
He could give us everything He has,
but what He is, we must earn for ourselves,
as we struggle to overcome adversity and gain
self-mastery. Our covenants help us to focus
our efforts to internalize His divine nature.
This is the purpose of the promises that
we make with Him. If it were not
possible to become as God is,
the necessity of covenants
would not make much
sense.

June 21

Above All
(1 Nephi 11:6)

He Who is **Above
All** teaches doctrine whose
curriculum is not secret, but rather
is sacred. If it suggests a shadowy ritual to
the uninitiated, it is because it is presented in a
language that cannot be learned in the ivory towers
of academia. Much of its liturgy, although inarticulate,
can be profoundly moving. Our education will expose
us to experience the infinite, along the ill-defined
terminator line between the temporal and
the eternal worlds. The workings and
ministrations of the Spirit, however,
will be of no interest to those
who dance in the spotlight
of a telestial stage.

June 22

Blessed God
(Alma 19:29)

The mysteries
of our **Blessed God** are
unfathomable to unenlightened minds
because they are spiritually discerned. They
articulate no formula for unrighteous dominion and
provide no protection from poor choices. They permit
no escape from consequences. They allow no justification
for rationalization, and cannot tolerate those who are
mesmerized by mediocre performance. They teach
economic, social, behavioral, political, and earth
sciences in ways that are alien to the
understanding of Spiritual
Babylon.

June 23

Blessed Jesus
(Alma 19:29)

As His work
is carried out, the
glory of **Blessed Jesus** will
rest upon His people. His doctrine
will be revealed in marvelous simplicity
and plainness. His Spirit will purge the stain of
sin from penitent hearts and will reveal all things.
His faithful disciples will receive their endowment of
power. Angels will watch over them, guide them, and
protect them. The kingdom will roll forth, and stakes
will be organized so that the elect may be gathered.
The walls of Babylon will crumble and fall, and
scattered Israel, the Lord's covenant people,
will learn the truth and rejoice in the
knowledge of their Savior, as the
waste places are built up
and become fruitful
vineyards.

June 24

Born of a Woman
(Alma 19:13)

Jesus was **Born of a Woman** who found favor before God. Mary strengthened her Son both temporally and spiritually, so that He might grow to manhood with a more sure witness of His divine mission. In comparison, Sir Isaac Newton accumulated an astonishing list of accomplishments that changed our physical world. Asked how he was able to do it all, he replied that he had stood on the shoulders of giants. What is the moral of the story? Perhaps it is that when we receive a little help from our friends, and moreover are blessed to experience the awesome positive influence of our mothers, we have the potential to tower over all of our contemporaries.

June 25

Branch of the Lord
(2 Nephi 14:2)

When we embrace the **Branch of the Lord**, oases will spring up in the desert, and living water will slake the thirst of a people eager for its life sustaining influence. The Lord will comfort and succor the families of the Saints and all of their sick and afflicted with the Bread of Life and the Balm of Gilead. His kingdom will fill the earth, and will propitiously occupy the void created when His terrible and swift sword overthrows powers, principalities, and false priests who oppress.

June 26

King Immanuel
(Doctrine & Covenants 128:22)

The gate may
be strait, and the way
narrow, but those who accept
King Immanuel as their guide will
find it within their reach to travel a path
of eternal progression by threading the eye
of the needle and walking a fine line past
the seemingly inexorable, unrelenting,
unstoppable, unavoidable, and
unalterable demands of
disproportion.

June 27

Christ - for so shall He be Called
(Mosiah 15:21)

At the close of the Apostolic Ministry, the noxious weeds of the apostasy were scattered about by the dry winds of a famine in the land for hearing the words of the Lord. The early Saints looked forward to the return of **Christ – for so shall He be Called**, with great anticipation. However, they had been taught that there must first be a long night of darkness from which there would be an Awakening, a Rebirth, a Renaissance, followed by a Reformation, then an Enlightenment, and finally a glorious Restoration of Truth.

June 28

Christ, the Lord God Omnipotent
(Mosiah 5:15)

The Old Testament might read more like The Book of Mormon, were it not for the plain and most precious parts relating to **Christ, the Lord God Omnipotent**, that have been taken away from that sacred record. Instead, because of the dilution of doctrine, a travesty has been made of many basic biblical teachings, to the end that many stumble for hearing the words of the Lord, insomuch that Satan has great power over them.

June 29

Christ the Lord
(Mosiah 16:15)

Ignorance of the fundamental
doctrines of **Christ the Lord** can be
at the root of apostasy from the truth.
Today, even some members of the Church
suffer from a shallow understanding of basic
principles of the Gospel. Consequently, the devil
seizes upon their weaknesses. Because he know who
the Lord's disciples are, they are all marked men and
women. They require a solid foundation of doctrinal
understanding, special priesthood protection, an
endowment of spiritual power received only in
the Lord's House, a blessing and setting apart
by file leaders, the prayers of the faithful,
and firm and abiding testimonies of
the divine authenticity of the
principles of the Plan of
Salvation, and of
its Author.

June 30

Christ
the Son
(Alma 11:44)

As
they struggle
to elucidate their
consideration of Christ,
well-meaning individuals
sometimes multiply mirrors and
manipulate angles without increasing
the light. Even a superficial study of the
activities of the architects of the Reformation
reveals that their common purpose was to
rediscover the power of **Christ the Son**
and revitalize the Church with an
infusion of His influence.

July 1

Christ, Who has Broken the Bands of Death
(Mosiah 15:23)

The
smoldering hatred
of apostasy sometimes
bursts into flames that have
been fueled by fear and fanned by the
winds of intolerance, ignorance, prejudice
and narrow-mindedness. The resulting fragility
of the pathways through which inspiration flows is
the alarming sign of a self-defeating illness that, if it is left
untreated, will effectively cripple the capacity to respond to
Christ, Who has Broken the Bands of Death. When barriers
to revealed communication from heaven have been thrown
up and the word of God is esteemed as a thing of naught,
faithlessness and conscious non-conformity to the
simple principles of the Gospel will propel the
stubborn and the headstrong on an
accelerating downward spiral
straight into the gaping
mouth of hell.

July 2

The Condescension of God
(1 Nephi 11:26)

The Condescension of God provides a way for us to face our challenges squarely. So when we have time to spare, we remember to ponder and pray rather than wander and play. If things do not seem to be going our way, we fall back on our eternal perspective. We use a cosmic yardstick to measure our progress. Our only recreational drug of choice is endorphins. We make extraordinary efforts to positively influence those situations over which we retain some control. We learn to accept that which we cannot change, but at the same time we create reservoirs of positive energy upon which we may draw in times of need.

July 3

The Father
of all Things
(Mosiah 7:27)

The Father of all Things blesses us with the capacity to meet our physical challenges as the years pass. In anticipation of these, we establish fitness programs tailored to our individual needs that are designed to help us maintain higher levels of health. We view our physical limitations positively, as opportunities to develop patience and perspective. We regularly re-evaluate our adherence to the spirit of the Word of Wisdom, and commit ourselves to goals of improvement based upon obedience to its principles.

July 4

A
Fire
(2 Nephi 20:17)

A Fire
that burns within
teaches what is best for
ourselves and for the Kingdom
of God, kindles our testimony of what
should be, and then energizes us to work with
all our capacity to make it happen, whatever the
cost might be. Then, when we are so richly
blessed far beyond the measure that we
deserve, the price, once so painfully
paid, is recalled in gladness.
We receive full
value.

July 5

A
Flame
(2 Nephi 20:17)

When we alienate ourselves from the **Flame** that is God's influence, we die spiritually because our eternal progression is halted. "Broad is the gate," taught the Savior, "and wide the way that leadeth to the deaths; and many there are that go in thereat, because they receive me not, neither do they abide in my law." (D&C 132:25). God measures our lives by watching how we behave when we are left to our own devices, after having received instruction regarding what we ought to do.

July 6

He is Full of Grace and Truth
(2 Nephi 2:6)

He is Full of Grace and Truth, and He intentionally gives us service opportunities, precisely because our time always seems to be at such a premium. We consistently discipline ourselves to make time to minister to the needs of our own families, to individuals outside our families, and to the Church. We trust in His protection when we consciously and deliberately put ourselves at risk as we venture out into the world to reclaim lost sheep. We fully commit ourselves to sustained efforts to contribute in positive ways to the welfare of our communities, regions, nations, and the world.

July 7

The God and Rock of their Salvation
(Jacob 7:25)

Possibly
the most significant
difference that accounts for
the superiority of the doctrine of **The
God and Rock of their Salvation** over any
other lifestyle is the process whereby the Gospel
of Jesus Christ is internalized by His disciples.
This phenomenon has been described as
sanctification by the Spirit, which is
more often an on-going process,
rather than something that
occurs at a specific
point in time.

July 8

God is Mindful of every People
(Alma 26:37)

The Lord in heaven Who is our **God is Mindful of every People**, even those of us who face character challenges. We are alert to the marginalization of our behavior, and so we learn to appreciate experiences that teach us humility, and we look forward with anticipation to those that confront our established paradigm. We attempt to so live that we would be happy to give our parrot to the town gossip. We try to be the kind of people that our dogs believe us to be. We commit the 13 Articles of Faith to life as well as to memory, and make them the tangible particles of our faith.

July 9

God
is with Us
(Alma 56:46)

God is with Us
when we are honest,
true, chaste, benevolent,
virtuous, and do good deeds.
As our faith increases, so does our
capacity to allow Him to guide us in all
aspects of our lives. We learn to recognize
and accept the suffering that is a part of life, and
strive to see adversity as a necessary and beneficial
feature of our experience. In our trials, we remember
the Savior Who is our Exemplar, and Who descended
beneath all things. We shun the shadows and instead
are drawn to His light. As we immerse ourselves in
the tangible element of the Spirit, we bask in its
glorious influence. It becomes our nature to
relate to all that is lovely, of good report,
and praiseworthy. We seek after that
which creates an atmosphere
that may be conducive to
improvement.

July 10

The God of Israel, Who is the Lord of Hosts
(1 Nephi 20:2)

We live in a society where ponder and pray have largely been replaced with wander and play. **The God of Israel, Who is the Lord of Hosts**, loves to hear us express both our petitions and our thanks in prayer. And so, we focus on the positive and overlook the shortcomings of others, because there is so much in ourselves that needs attention. We aim for specificity in our prayers, ask questions, acknowledge answers, articulate why we are thankful, and orient ourselves toward repentance. Purposeful prayer can help us to maintain a constant state of improvement leading to perfection.

July 11

A God of Miracles
(2 Nephi 28:6)

Authority that has been exercised through the use of violent or coercive means is a poor substitute for leadership or power. As a matter of fact, they are mutually exclusive. Where one is present, the other is absent. **A God of Miracles** warns us about the satanic inclination to abuse authority, especially by those who have it, but are least prepared for positions of trust and responsibility. He has provided an endowment that underpins the principle that the Plan of Salvation operates more by addition than by subtraction.

July 12

The God of Nature
(1 Nephi 18:12)

One of the terrible consequences of the world's fascination with Babylon and of the adoption of its lifestyle is a spiritual insensitivity born of competition between individuals. Win or lose seems to be the prevailing standard. At best, we learn in business that you don't get what you deserve, you get what you negotiate. Daddy Warbucks illustrated the worst in us, when he told Annie that "you don't have to be nice to those you climb over, or step on, on your way up the ladder of success, if you don't plan on coming back down again." But **The God of Nature** said: "Whosoever will be chief among you, let him be your servant." (Matthew 20:27).

July 13

The God of our Fathers
(1 Nephi 19:10)

Unlike an indulgent parent, **The God of our Fathers** doesn't give us that which we don't deserve, nor does He submit to our pressure to impart to us that which we do not need. So, we resolve not to act like spoiled children in our prayers. We communicate with Him as we would with our own fathers. Through His prophet, He revealed: "And whoso receiveth not my voice is not acquainted with my voice, and is not of me." (D&C 84:52). If we pray always and don't lose faith, God directs our performance in such a way that it is therapeutic for our souls.

July 14

God will Deliver Us
(Alma 58:37)

76% of all Americans identify themselves as Christian, while 36% attend church on a weekly basis. Only 9% report that religion is the most important aspect of their life. It's hard to say how many Americans repent on a regular basis, but we could probably take a cue from how things are going. **God will Deliver Us** and we will prosper in the land, as long as we strive to keep the commandments and we speedily repent when we have failed to do so. Otherwise, we have no promise. God will continue to bless this land only for as long as its inhabitants repent!

July 15

Great Mediator of all Men
(2 Nephi 2:27)

The very first condition of happiness is a clear conscience. Before even a scratch can heal, it has to be clean. Anyone who has had dirt vigorously scrubbed out of an ugly wound knows how thoroughly the task must be performed before a sterile dressing may be applied to allow the healing process to begin. The same principle applies to repentance. The **Great Mediator of all Men** stands ready to purify our souls, but there can be no skeletons lurking in the closet, and He makes no allowances for dry rot. We cannot superficially whitewash our sins to cover them up. Before He can do a complete home makeover, our habitation must be dismantled right down to its stud walls.

July 16

A
Great Spirit
(Alma 18:26)

The
purpose of our
mortal experience is to
increase in stature, until we
have assumed both the image and
likeness of God, Who is **A Great Spirit**.
During the process of this transformation,
we will fail again and again in our efforts. This
creates a problem, because no unclean thing can
dwell with God, and yet it is human nature to
violate the commandments. Sin is like sand
in our gears that will cause our forward
momentum to come to a grinding halt.
God, however, has provided the
principle of repentance, as a
healing machine oil, so
that we may yet
be holy.

July 17

The
Great Spirit
(Alma 18:3)

The great blessing of repentance is that it allows us to become clean in the sight of God, so that we can get moving again on the pathway to perfection. After repentance, **The Great Spirit** will remember our sins no more. It is true that we might retain a recollection of them, insofar as they increase our testimonies, strengthen us to become more stalwart, and better prepare us to positively influence others. But we will no longer feel the guilt, or experience the withdrawal of the Spirit, that is so painfully associated with our unresolved transgression of the law.

July 18

This Great Spirit, Who is God
(Alma 18:28)

When our hearts
have been hardened against
the messages of salvation, it is as
though our portion is diminished further
and further, until we find ourselves defenseless
against the aggressive tactics of the devil. In the hard
light of day, left to our own devices, our exercise of agency
in the midst of difficult choices and opposition can lead us
to a conundrum of cosmic proportions with devastating
consequences. Without the protection of **This Great
Spirit, Who is God**, we are influenced, not by the
illuminating truths of our Master, but by the
vulgar lies of the deceiver, who moves into
the void created by our obstinacy, with
the intention of catching us in
his snares, and dragging
us down to hell.

July 19

That Great Spirit, Who knows all Things
(Alma 18:18)

Because we have been given the Light of Christ, we all feel the presence of **That Great Spirit, Who knows all Things**, and we instinctively acknowledge our God-given character traits of intrinsic goodness and the capacity to recognize and cleave to truth. Joseph Smith confidently said of the Saints: "I teach them correct principles, and they govern themselves." Such knowledge is powerful, and will forever govern ignorance. If, with the help of God, we mean to determine our own fate, we must fortify ourselves with His wisdom.

July 20

He Shall be Called by the Name of Christ
(Mosiah 5:9)

The Redeemer of Israel **Shall be Called by the Name of Christ**. It is because of our love for Him that we feel sorrow for our sins. We feel terrible about them. We feel profoundly filthy and want nothing more than to unload and abandon them. We are almost obsessive-compulsive about cleansing our souls. We are broken in heart, and contrition prepares us to receive the things of the Spirit. When our faith has convicted us of our sins, we are prepared to ask, as did those on the Day of Pentecost: "What shall we do?" When we receive the answer, we marvel at its simplicity and the easiness of the way, because we are already moving along on the road that has been defined by the first principles and ordinances of the Gospel.

July 21

He Shall be Called the Son of God
(Mosiah 15:2)

We surely do
not have all the answers,
but we do know to Whom we
may look for redemption, and that our
Savior **Shall be Called the Son of God**. We
share more common ground with Him, and with
others, than we realize. Humans have a genome of
about three billion DNA nucleotides. We differ from
each other in approximately one in a thousand of
these, about one tenth of one percent. There are
about three million nucleotide differences
between two random human beings, but
there are about two billion nine
hundred ninety seven million
that are identical. These
are the traits that bind
us together.

July 22

He that Hath Cut Rahab
(2 Nephi 8:9)

He that Hath Cut Rahab
has endorsed a Plan that allows
us to overcome the world, to attain
His stature and become all that He now
is. It shows us how to incorporate into our
own nature and being His image and likeness.
In the process of being Born Again, our corruptible
bodies become clean and pure, and infused with light.
It is critical to the success of the Plan that the bodies we
were given when we came to this earth be kept in good
condition, because they are all we've got. They are the
designated tabernacles of our spirits. They came from
God, and will eventually be presented to Him when
we stand before His throne to be judged. He can
tolerate no dents, nicks, or scratches, nor even
normal wear-and-tear on our moving parts.
He requires that we return to Him as
we were sent forth. He demands
nothing less than
perfection.

July 23

Him that Bringeth Good Tidings
(Mosiah 15:18)

Recurring repentance and rededication to our baptismal covenants release us from the bondage of sin, and qualify us to enjoy the blessings reserved for the faithful. This level of commitment will allow us to overcome the limitations of the flesh and to position ourselves to reach our potential. It will also unleash the powers of heaven in our behalf, break the bands of death, and throw open the gates of the Celestial Kingdom. A spiritual transformation will take place in our lives as we live the Celestial Law of **Him that Bringeth Good Tidings**.

July 24

His
Word
(2 Nephi 19:8)

Our
acquisition of
faith in **His Word** may be
compared to the act of driving
a screw in to a solid piece of wood.
With each turn, the grip is more secure,
until ultimately, when the screw is all the
way in, the anchor is trustworthy. The screw
cannot be easily removed unless fear replaces
faith, turn by turn, loosening the hold. When
the screw is flush, however, and the fastener
of faith is sure, it is not dormant. The same
amount of energy that had aforetime been
required to firmly position the screw can
now be directed elsewhere, with an
equally profitable result, even as
the product of that initial
expenditure of faith
remains.

July 25

Holy God
(2 Nephi 9:39)

When we have
completed the painful process
of repentance, the Plan of Salvation
shifts into high gear and the Atonement takes
command of every situation. The unique source
of peace that has been promised by the Savior is our
complete and all-encompassing dependence upon the
inherent power of the sacrifice of our **Holy God**, leading
to our Heavenly Father's consequent forgiveness of our
sins. The reconciliation between cherubim and a flaming
sword typifies the intervention of Mercy to satisfy the
demands of Justice. This symbolic description of
the intangible elements leading to salvation
is vividly and prominently portrayed
in the scriptures.

July 26

Holy, Holy God
(Alma 31:15)

There is a heavenly counterpart to the names by which we are known on the earth. In His Church, we are called by the name of Jesus Christ in a familial way. We are the children of a **Holy, Holy God** in the sense that He has united our bodies and spirits through the Resurrection: "For this day He hath spiritually begotten you," explained Benjamin. (Mosiah 5:7). There is a special family relationship reserved for the faithful that compounds the reality that we are the spirit children of our Father. It is our privilege to know that we are the acorns of a mighty oak, and that our autobiographical thread leads all the way back to Him.

July 27

I am a God of Miracles
(2 Nephi 27:23)

Associated blessings always accompany obedience to specific commandments. These rewards are sometimes temporal but are always spiritual. Now and then, we recognize the eternal immutability of that grand principle, but in general, we do not. However, as we come to a greater appreciation of the Plan of Salvation and of the covenants made at the altars of the temple, and as we begin to understand the nature of God by visiting His house frequently, we will see with greater clarity and appreciate more broadly that our Savior is truly a **God of Miracles** Who touches our lives in intimate ways on a daily basis.

July 28

I am He that Comforteth You
(2 Nephi 8:12)

**I am He
that Comforteth
You** has provided a refuge
that is untainted from the blood and
sins of this generation, where you may flee
from Spiritual Babylon. It is a place for you to
shelter your spirit, grasp the horns of sanctuary,
quiet your racing heart, and ease the tensions
resulting from life in the fast lane. There
are times and places where you can
calmly reflect on the quality
of your preparation to
live with Him
eternally.

July 29

I the Lord thy God am a Jealous God
(Mosiah 13:13)

The Lord our **God is a Jealous God**. He has a vested interest in our welfare, and watches over us as would "a hen (who) doth gather her brood under her wings" (Luke 13:34) because He would like us to become reacquainted with Him. If that seems intimidating, we can repetitively practice in anticipation of that reunion by employing Gospel principles as we develop good habit patterns. Ultimately, we will have internalized the celestial qualities designed by the Plan to allow us to enjoy His company. We can begin now by achieving perfection in our repentance, so that we may feel in greater abundance the stirrings of His love and concern for us.

July 30

I was in the Beginning with the Father, and am the Firstborn
(Doctrine & Covenants 93:21)

The Savior declared: **I was in the Beginning with the Father, and am the Firstborn**. He revealed a foundation principle of self-mastery when He told Joseph Smith: "I, the Lord, will forgive whom I will forgive, but of you it is required to forgive all men." (D&C 64:10). Brigham Young put it a little more bluntly when he declared: "He who takes offense when none was intended is a fool, and he who takes offense when one was intended is usually a fool." We can only be fully repentant when we are strictly obedient to the principle of forgiveness, and that door swings both ways.

July 31

I am He; I am the First, and I am also the Last
(1 Nephi 20:12)

The pure
love of Christ, of
Him Who is **the First and
also the Last**, is all-encompassing,
and is built upon a foundation of faith
and hope. It is the supreme characteristic
of every determined disciple. Mormon taught
that if we are "meek and lowly in heart, and
confess by the power of the Holy Ghost
that Jesus is the Christ," with a sure
hope born of faith, we "must
needs have charity."
(Moroni 7:44).

August 1

Jesus Christ,
the Son of God
(2 Nephi 25:19)

When we
live in thanksgiving,
are perfect in our repentance,
and love ourselves, our fellowmen, and
Jesus Christ, the Son of God, we will see the
glass as half full. No matter what life may throw
at us, we will put a positive spin on our experiences.
Love, together with its companion virtue of compassion,
will overpower our carnal nature, with its malevolent
envy, petty jealousies, and malignant prejudices,
and lift us stratospherically into the rarified
atmosphere of heaven on earth.

August 2

I am Jesus Christ, the Son of God,
Who was Crucified for the Sins of the World
(Doctrine & Covenants 35:2)

With the words: **I am Jesus Christ, the Son of God, Who was Crucified for the Sins of the World** ringing in our ears, we perform acts of Quiet Christianity for which there is no recognition, recompense, or thought of reciprocation. The first five books of the Old Testament speak of keeping the Sabbath day holy just once, but of serving our neighbors thirty times. When we seek to nurture the best in others, we somehow bring out what is good in ourselves.

August 3

I,
the Lord
(1 Nephi 20:15)

Our
gratitude
knows no bounds
when we realize that **the
Lord** loves us so much that,
without our conscious awareness,
He sends strangers among us,
as angels from heaven,
to minister to our
needs.

August 4

In the Beginning the Word was, for He was the
Word, even the Messenger of Salvation
(Doctrine & Covenants 93:8)

**In the Beginning
the Word was, for He was the
Word, even the Messenger of Salvation.**
When we follow Him, we undertake the ultimate
incredible journey that empowers us to become what
we had heretofore scarcely dreamed possible. It may be the
road less traveled, with many doctrinal detours, telestial
traffic jams, and conceptual cul-de-sacs threatening to
lead us astray, but the rewards along the way,
and at our final destination, make our
perseverance in enduring to the
end worth the effort.

August 5

The Only Begotten of the Father, Full of Grace and Truth, even the Spirit of Truth
(Doctrine & Covenants 93:11)

Our repentance leading to forgiveness is made possible by the tender mercies of **The Only Begotten of the Father,** Who is **Full of Grace and Truth, even the Spirit of Truth.** Only His Atonement can remove all traces of soul-stain from the threads of the beautiful and vibrant tapestry that is woven into our sinews. That record is written in the tablets of the mind. It is our coat of many colors, and it cannot lie. In a coming day, it will be unfolded for the examination of God in heaven.

August 6

I am Jesus Christ, Who cometh Quickly,
in an Hour you Think Not
(Doctrine & Covenants 51:20)

**Jesus Christ,
Who cometh Quickly,
in an Hour you Think Not**,
watches with sadness when His
children cater to the lowest common
denominator of behavior. He wonders
how they can think that the results of their
meager efforts could possibly be stratospheric.
When the bar has been lowered so drastically
that even the most morally challenged
individuals can easily step over it,
should olympian outcomes or
oscar-worthy performances
really be expected?

August 7

I am the Lord your God,
dwelling in Zion, My
Holy Mountain
(Joel 3:17)

The
Savior revealed:
**I am the Lord your
God, dwelling in Zion,
My Holy Mountain**. Faith
in Him intensifies our desire
to repent, so we may qualify to
reside with Him in the Holy City.
In the meantime, our efforts to
maintain temple worthiness
put our lives in harmony
with Gospel principles,
and position us to
sustain forward
momentum.

August 8

The Lord will roar from Zion, and utter His Voice from Jerusalem
(Amos 1:2)

In the Last Days, as we face relentless challenges to morality, **The Lord will roar from Zion, and utter His Voice from Jerusalem**. The raw sewage that permeates our culture has contaminated the understanding of inspired counsel, and a raging current of filth has undermined the foundations of its appreciation. Chaste behavior requires a great deal of faith, since the lifestyle of self-restraint is almost universally disparaged by a vocal majority that dismisses it as an anachronism. But the more the world indulges, the more it has to lose. The more it abstains, the more it has to gain.

August 9

Jesus Christ, your Lord and your
God, and your Redeemer
(Doctrine & Covenants 18:47)

In all things,
walk circumspectly before
the Lord, that you might be blessed
and guided by His Holy Spirit. Humble
yourself with a conscious awareness of your
own shortcomings, failings, and imperfections,
that you might be led to total reliance on
the merits of **Jesus Christ, your
Lord and your God, and
your Redeemer.**

August 10

Jesus,
Thou Son of God
(Alma 36:18)

If security may
be found in abstinence,
then its adherents must have the
satisfaction of a freedom that others
do not enjoy. Self-mastery releases us
from bondage to bad habits, compulsion,
and sin, that clouds our vision with an
opacity that obstructs our ability to
see what is really there. Those
who are chaste are provided
with a medium of clarity
allowing them to rely
upon the merits
of **Jesus** the
Son of
God.

August 11

A
Just God
(Alma 29:4)

Alma realized that
the poor Zoramites were
fortunate because their difficult
circumstances compelled them to
be humble. He discerned that if they
received priesthood directed Gospel
instruction, **A Just God** would bless
them with faith unto repentance,
that would lead to sanctification
by the Spirit and forgiveness
via the ordinances of the
Gospel, thereby paving
the way for their
salvation by
grace.

August 12

A Life
which is Endless
(Mosiah 16:9)

When we
honor our covenants,
our obedience infuses us
with the priesthood and spiritual
power necessary to overcome evil and
obtain exaltation in the enjoyment of **A Life
which is Endless**. Joseph Smith said that
our salvation consists of being placed
beyond the power of the enemies of
our progression, such as lying,
greediness, immorality,
and other vices.

August 13

Your Light
in the Wilderness
(1 Nephi 17:13)

We live in
a world in which
the distinctions between
good and evil are blurred, and
idolatry takes an ephemeral form,
like a will-o-the-wisp. We try to focus
on something, anything, that will provide
the stability that so eludes us. Whether it is a
sex goddess, eternal youth, free love, or the siren
song of enchantment from a glossy magazine cover,
it is all the same. Many years ago, one of our most
popular periodicals was "Life." Then there was
"People," and then "Us." Next was "Self." We
might ask: "Where do we go from there?"
The answer should be: "Do not stop,
even to cancel your subscription.
Go directly to **Your Light
in the Wilderness**."

August 14

My Fortress and my Deliverer
(2 Samuel 2:22)

My Fortress and my Deliverer stands before me in bold counterpoint to the inevitable sense of abandonment that is felt by those whose misplaced trust in the adversary has left them with neither root nor branch. The Lord's grand principle of reconciliation stems a rising tide of raw sewage consisting of empty despair, hopelessness, despondency, and misery, that is nothing more than nauseating effluent left behind as Satan slithers by.

August 15

Advocate
(1 John 2:1)

At the last day, when we make our appearance to be judged, our **Advocate** will have enough fire-power in His arsenal to deal with our worst depravities, moral corruption, and degradation. But let us never forget that He also atoned for our every day garden-variety sins. We have Him on retainer, and so He stands ready to plead our case at the Bar of Justice when either our felony or our misdemeanor offenses are brought to trial.

August 16

The
Truth of God
(2 Nephi 28:28)

The Truth of God may be our best friend, but He will not always be there to reassure us that all is well in Zion, or that prosperity lies just around the corner. Affirmations are fine, as long as we take them with a grain of salt. It is better to be warned about the calamities and difficulties that are a part of life, as well as those that come as the result of our disobedience to proven principles, and then to take obligatory remedial steps.

August 17

My Deliverer and my Shield
(Psalms 144:2)

In 1921,
President Heber J. Grant
issued a prophetic warning to
the world, concerning the conscious
persecution of Israel, the covenant people
of the Lord. He declared: "By the authority of the
Holy Priesthood of God, that has again been restored
to the earth, and by the ministration, under the direction
of the Prophet of God, Apostles of the Lord Jesus Christ
have been to the Holy Land and have dedicated that
country for the return of the Jews; and we believe
that in the due time of the Lord they shall be in
the favor of God again. And let no Latter-day
Saint be guilty of taking any part in any
crusade against these people." Truly,
could the Jews say: Jehovah is **My
Deliverer and my Shield**. Latter
day Saints are ardent Zionists
who stand with the Jews in
their struggle to survive
as a people and as
a nation.

August 18

The Lord God, the God of Abraham, the God of Isaac, and the God of Jacob
(Alma 29:11)

Because of the
ministry and martyrdom
of Joseph Smith and others, faith
has increased to the point that the ancient
covenant made by **The Lord God, the God of Abraham, the God of Isaac and the God of Jacob**
has now been re-established. It is now possible for
the fulness of the Gospel to be proclaimed by the
weak and unlearned disciples of Christ unto the
ends of the earth, and before kings, rulers, and
magistrates. The strength of their message
is its doctrine, which will bear up
under the careful scrutiny of
even the most powerful
minds on earth.

August 19

The Lord is Near
(2 Nephi 7:8)

The first principle
of the Gospel to which most
seekers of truth are exposed is faith
in the Lord Jesus Christ, but repentance
can also be a powerful teacher, reassuring
us that **The Lord is Near**. Without faith, we
lead one-dimensional lives that have no depth
or breadth. But when our faith leads us to repent,
we develop across many planes of experience, and
we delight in hope for a better world. We become
firm, steadfast, and immoveable. Our expanding
awareness becomes a springboard that vaults
us directly to the ordinances of baptism and
the receipt of the gift of the Holy Ghost
that are the result of the sustained
effort that follows faith and is
the reward of repentance.

August 20

The Lord
is with Thee
(1 Nephi 17:55)

With an unflagging positive mental attitude, Ebenezer's young nephew said: "I never knew my mother. But I hope to know Scrooge one day." (Dickens, "A Christmas Carol"). When **The Lord is with Thee**, you will come to know your Father in Heaven. That experience will open up unimagined possibilities realting to family exaltation.

August 21

The Lord of Hosts is My Name
(2 Nephi 8:15)

When we have exercised our agency, two conditions immediately become obvious: the opportunity to make choices in an atmosphere of opposition, and the necessity of facing consequences that are associated with those decisions. The urgency of reconciliation to the laws of heaven through Atonement is not so readily apparent, but is equally important. **The Lord of Hosts is My Name** waits on our initiative.

August 23

The Lord our God, Who has Redeemed us and Made us Free
(Alma 58:41)

Too often, our
interactions with others
are "anti-enemy" rather than
"pro-Gospel, in the sense that Latter-
day Saints sometimes retreat into defensive
postures when confronted by those who question
their beliefs. **The Lord our God, Who has Redeemed
us and Made us Free**, teaches that adversarial
relationships do not foster understanding or
appreciation of the more prevalent
similarities that exist within the
various belief systems that
are embraced by His
children.

August 22

The Most High God,
Possessor of Heaven and Earth
(Genesis 14:19)

Steady illumination
from the Light of Christ
is designed to lead us to truth,
and ultimately to **The Most High
God**, Who is the **Possessor of Heaven
and Earth**. When it motivates us to sow
the seeds of inquiry in the fertile Gospel soil
that has been provided for our benefit, meekness
and humility are germinated, and we can expect to
reap a bountiful harvest of blessings that are related
to these virtues. Even the quality of endurance, as we
pass through the refiner's fire on our way to personal
rediscovery and enlightenment, can be quite pleasant
and positive, and give us a great deal of satisfaction,
although its cultivation frequently comes at
a heavy performance cost.

August 24

The Lord your God, even Alpha and Omega, the Beginning and the End, Whose Course is One Eternal Round, the Same Today as Yesterday, and Forever, your God and your Redeemer
(Doctrine & Covenants 35:1)

We fervently
believe in **The Lord
(our) God, even Alpha and
Omega, the Beginning and the
End, Whose Course is One Eternal
Round, the Same Today as Yesterday,
and Forever (our) God and (our) Redeemer**.
The 13 Articles of Faith define our dogma, but
they also emphasize the differences that exist
between ourselves and our Christian friends.
They constitute the catechism that sets us
apart as Latter-day Saints. We may
invite criticism if we emphasize
these differences, rather than
focusing on our many
similarities.

August 25

The Lord your God, even Jesus Christ, the Great I Am, Alpha and Omega, the Beginning and the End, the Same which Looked upon the Wide Expanse of Eternity, and all the Seraphic Hosts of Heaven, before the World was made
(Doctrine & Covenants 38:1)

We are passionate in our faith and testimony that "children are an heritage of the Lord, and the fruit of the womb is (our) reward." (Psalms 127:3). But we go one step further. "Little children are," in fact, "holy, being sanctified through the atonement of Jesus Christ." (D&C 74:7). We acknowledge, emphasize, and celebrate the innocence of children, a doctrine that has been affirmed, and reaffirmed, by **The Lord your God, even Jesus Christ, the Great I Am, Alpha and Omega, the Beginning and the End, the Same which Looked upon the Wide Expanse of Eternity, and all the Seraphic Hosts of Heaven, before the World was made.**

August 26

Merciful
is our God
(Alma 24:15)

Every
discussion of faith must
distinguish it from its caricatures. It
is not naiveté, nor is it wishful thinking
or gullibility. It is more than confidence and
greater than optimism. Faith and positive thinking
go hand in hand, but faith is much more powerful than
attitude. However **Merciful is our God**, heavenly signs
cannot generate faith. In fact, we should not desire signs,
because faith precedes the miracle. During the genesis
of faith, it may be necessary to take a few steps into
the darkness, before the Spirit reveals the identity
of its Author and Finisher. After our faith has
been tried, it may be confirmed by direct
experience. In any case, the way before
us will be bathed in its spiritual
strong searchlight, and we
will walk in its light.

August 27

I, the Lord, am Merciful and Gracious unto Those who Fear Me, and Delight to Honor those who Serve me in Righteousness and in Truth unto the End
(Doctrine & Covenants 76:5)

My grandmother
may not have thought
of herself as a disciple of Christ.
I do not believe she ever realized that
**the Lord is Merciful and Gracious unto
Those who Fear** Him, **and Delight(s) to Honor
those who Serve** Him **in Righteousness and in Truth
unto the End.** She didn't own a well-worn Bible, and
was not well-acquainted with the Savior's life and
teachings, but she intuitively followed His
example. She committed His admonition
not to memory but to life: "Inasmuch
as ye have done it unto one of the
least of these my brethren, ye
have done it unto me."
(Matthew 25.40).

August 28

Mightier than all the Earth
(1 Nephi 4:1)

Priesthood power
generates the opportunity
for dynamic change, as knowledge
flows along established channels created by
One Who is **Mightier than all the Earth**. At the
same time, personal accountability, responsibility,
and commitment to obedience increase. The desire to
serve strengthens the bonds of brotherhood, removes
obstacles that stand in the way of understanding,
and creates an interdependent community of
believers that crosses cultural lines and
breaks down the economic, social,
and political barriers that exist
among people of different
backgrounds.

August 29

He is Mightier than I
(1 Nephi 10:8)

Giving myself to
One Who is **Mightier
than I** has required a revision
of the commonly accepted standards
of qualification that were drilled into
me during my secular schooling. I
have learned that in the Kingdom
of God, it is availability, and
not ability or inability,
that is important.

August 30

My God
(2 Nephi 4:20)

The
principles of
the Gospel are like the
stars on a celestial horizon,
and I navigate through life by
using them to take my bearings on
eternity. I know that the wind and the
waves are always on the side of the ablest
navigator. Enthusiasm can be defined as "a
prophetic frenzy, possession by a god, or
supernatural inspiration." To be most
effective and life-directing, my own
personal mission statement has
been crafted so that it reflects
my enthusiasm for
My God.

August 31

One Eternal Round, the Same Today as Yesterday and Forever, your God
(Doctrine & Covenants 35:1)

Under ideal circumstances, as we mature in the Gospel and gain spiritual maturity, "by doing our duty, our faith increases until it becomes perfect knowledge." (Heber J. Grant). The Savior is **One Eternal Round, the Same Today as Yesterday and Forever, your God**. Certainly, He is full of faith, and yet He is omniscient. There is nothing that He does not know. For our part, as imperfect mortals struggling to believe what we do not see, the reward of our maturing faith is to see what we believe. Then, we will be faithful, or full of faith.

September 1

My
Great God
(Alma 24:8)

The
rational approach
of secular humanism is the
mortal enemy of faith. It and other
similar ideologies are devilish doctrines,
though their influence may be subtle. **My Great
God** finds them abominable because they substitute the
twisted theories of men for the expansive principles of the
Plan, and thereby thwart its execution in our behalf. These
philosophies have no life-generating or sustaining energy,
because they deny the nurturing influence of our Father
in Heaven. They are impotent because they have no
power to produce purposeful performance. They
may have the sizzle, but, upon closer inspection,
it becomes clear that they lack the steak.
They are all talk, and no show.

September 2

My
Name's Sake
(1 Nephi 20:9)

Spiritual
security has always
depended upon how we
live, not where we live or when
we live. When we make and keep
temple covenants with God, with
My Name's Sake, and we strive
throughout our lives to be
pure in heart, we help
to build Zion, a city
that transcends
time and
space.

September 3

My
Strength
(1 Nephi 21:5)

Eternal truth is
at the very foundation
of my faith, and is the catalyst
that motivates me to action. Truth
is deed. The horizon of my knowledge
and an appreciation of **My Strength**
extends only as far as my action.
This is why my works are an
important companion to
my vital, active
faith.

September 4

The Name of Christ, or of God
(Mosiah 25:23)

Those who
fight against Zion are
unfaithful to Gospel principles
and have thus prostituted themselves.
Such individuals and institutions have been
characterized as being "the whore of the earth"
in the sense that they are corrupt and are idol
worshipers. Those who will not take upon
themselves **The Name of Christ, or of
God**, often carry bullhorns and
picket signs. They may be
advocates for social
change, but they
are enemies
to God.

September 5

One Among you Whom ye Know Not
(1 Nephi 10:8)

The pure love of **One Among you Whom ye Know Not** is characterized by sensitivity toward others, and is more focused on celestial sureties and less on telestial uncertainties. It is humble and selfless, and reflects poise under provocation. It has no secret agenda to follow. It is repulsed by sin and is drawn toward the light, and is continually open to that which is good. It naturally follows prayer and repentance. It is within the reach of all of us. It is God's love, or charity.

September 6

There is but One God
(Alma 11:35)

Not
by knowledge,
but by our faith we come
to the realization that **There is
but One God.** If we did not believe in
the Lord Jesus Christ, if we had no faith in
Him or in the power of His Atonement, we would
be inclined to pay little heed to His commandments.
It is because we have that faith that we are brought
into harmony with His truth and have a desire
in our hearts to follow Him wherever
that path may take us.

September 7

They are One God
(Mosiah 15:4)

The speciality of
today's charismatic leaders is
to capitalize on our distress, bang
the drums of war, and whip us into a
nationalistic fervor. We allow their rhetoric to
reach a fever pitch, causing our blood to boil with
prejudice, suspicion, doubt, misgivings, mistrust, and
even hatred of those whom we have not taken the time to
understand. We face the spectre of voluntarily surrendering
our rights and responsibilities to leaders who realize they
will not need to work very hard to consolidate their
authority, concentrate their power, and usurp our
privileges. Infused with a fear that is fueled by
a frenzied media, we give up our rights to the
highest bidder or to the loudest and most
persistent jingoist. In these situations,
we need to be still, and remember
that **They are One God** Who
control our destiny.

September 8

One
Messiah
(2 Nephi 25:18)

Our
circumstances
are tailored by our Father
to meet our needs, and the sacrifices
we make along the way will be no less than
those of the men and women who established the
Church soon after its Restoration. So, this is not a time
to sit back and rest on our laurels. The work remains
to be done, and it is the same as it has always been:
To carry the light of the everlasting Gospel of
the **One Messiah** to "every nation,
kindred, tongue, and people."
(Mosiah 15:28).

September 9

The Only Begotten of the Father, Full of Grace, Equity, and Truth, Full of Patience Mercy, and Long-suffering
(Alma 9:26)

Satan
misleads and blinds
inexperienced or immature
Saints with clever caricatures of our
one true Comforter. The limitles spiritual
reserves of **The Only Begotten of the Father,
Full of Grace, Equity, and Truth, Full of Patience,
Mercy, and Long-suffering,** however, provide a
reservoir of counsel to help us to avoid being
deceived. The example of the Savior's
mortal ministry illuminates truths
concerning the way the Holy
Ghost can help us to more
fully enjoy His influence
and receive all of the
blessings of the
Gospel.

September 10

Our
Great God
(Alma 24:7)

The Savior
knew that our
sins would require
that Justice be satisfied, so
Our Great God stepped up to
the plate and paid an astronomical
price for our transgressions. His sacrifice
was literally out of this world. If we choose to
ignore the principle of Mercy that is triggered by
repentance and fulfilled in the Atonement, the burden
of proof of our innocence will fall upon us. On that day
of reckoning, when sentence is pronounced, we will be
found wanting. We will be vulnerable and exposed to
the demands of the law, and bear the burden of pain
and suffering that its violation requires. Perhaps
the harshest penalty in the justice system to
which we must all give credit is the
inability of the unrepentant to
receive a fulness of joy in
the resurrection.

September 11

The
Peace of God
(Alma 7:27)

**The
Peace of God**
encompasses all of the
ingredients of a Recipe for
Success, as well as instructions
concerning their proper use. The
tiny human beans created by our Father
are Gods in Embryo. All of the theology of
the Church can be boiled down to making the
journey to Christ, in being filled with His love,
and in conducting ourselves as the offspring
of Heavenly Parents. When we follow that
recipe, we become partners with Them
in Their work, which is to germinate
within each of us the power to
sprout and then to grow
to our own lush and
leafy spiritual
maturity.

September 12

The Redeemer
of all Men
(Alma 28:8)

If the
world does not
fall at the feet of **The
Redeemer of all Men**, it
is only because the spiritual
aether in which He is enveloped
is impenetrable to unprepared
minds.

September 13

My Rock and mine Everlasting God
(2 Nephi 4:35)

The Restoration of the
Gospel is an on-going production
begun by our forebearers, a continually
evolving epoch drama in which I am an eager
particpant. I realize how great is my reliance upon
My Rock and mine Everlasting God. I am only
His poor understudy, but with His guidance
and direction, I can be a card-carrying cast
member with the ability to mentor new
generations of Saints as they come to
know the Savior. I dare not pass up
this great opportunity to accept
such a wonderful role and
responsibility. It will be
my oscar-worthy
magnum opus.

September 14

The Rock from whence
ye are Hewn
(2 Nephi 8:1)

**The Rock from whence
ye are Hewn** facilitates unity
by providing for the administration of
ordinances that allow you to be organized
into an eternal family unit after you have entered
into the patriarchal order of marriage. This covenant is
consumated in the temple, where you learn the principles
of temporal and spiritual administration. In a sacred
assembly, you promise to consecrate your time
and talents to the Church and Kingdom
whose purpose and objective is to
make sure that families can
be together forever.

September 15

The Rock of my Righteousness
(2 Nephi 4:35)

In addition to its more obvious benefits, studying the life and times of **The Rock of my Righteousness** will also help me to become more disciplined. As my thoughts are illuminated, decision making becomes easier as the choices before me are clarified against a backdrop of Gospel principles that are applied in a real-world setting. I realize that I may achieve new heights through a union with the Holy Ghost that would have otherwise been unattainable.

September 16

The Salvation of the Lord
(1 Nephi 19:17)

Our lives can
be unpredictable and
full of uncertainty, but if our
footing is firm and our stability
secure, we will successfully adapt to
every circumstance, even as we maintain
our focus on **The Salvation of the Lord**. As
we continue our journey through mortality,
we begin to understand that experience
is only a prelude to the joy that will
be ours when we have arrived
at the pearly gates of our
celestial destination.

September 17

Salvation unto the
Ends of the Earth
(1 Nephi 21:6)

The mysteries of God
are those truths that can be
known only by revelation from the
Holy Ghost. When we hunger and thirst
after a comprehension of true principles and seek
Salvation unto the Ends of the Earth in anticipation
of a spiritual feast, the doctrine of the priesthood
will distill upon our souls as the dew from
heaven and the Holy Ghost will be our
constant companion. By its power
we may discern the truth
of all things.

September 18

I am the Same that Spake unto you from the Beginning
(Doctrine & Covenants 8:12)

It may be
"A Wonderful Life,"
but if you are past feeling,
you are out of touch with God,
and any righteous desires you may
have had will be just beyond your reach as
their lucidity is lost in the cold fog of confusion,
uncertainty, hesitancy, and ambiguity. **The Same that Spake unto you from the Beginning** can
no longer guide you because you have used
your agency to unilaterally disrupt open
lines of communication that aforetime
existed. Just look at what happened
in Bedford Falls without the
virtuous influence of
George Bailey.

September 19

I am the Same which have taken
the Zion of Enoch into Mine own Bosom
(Doctrine & Covenants 38:4)

Like an eager
and hopeful child riding
a carousel, we must always be
prepared, and be ready to reach out
for the brass ring. We dare not become
sidetracked, or experiment with unproven
behavioral lifestyles of questionable value.
Tinkering with the elements of the Plan
jeopardizes our future. The guidance
of Him Who is **the Same which has
taken the Zion of Enoch into**
His **own Bosom** will work
as well in the Last Days
as it did in antiquity.

September 20

I am the same which Spake, and the world was Made, and all Things Came by Me
(Doctrine & Covenants 38:3)

The Savior said:
I am the same which Spake, and the world was Made, and all Things Came by Me, and so it is natural to pray for His guidance before sitting down with the scriptures. We slow down our minds and free ourselves from the cares and concerns of the world. As we read and our minds are illuminated, we continue to pray for understanding. We keep writing material handy, in anticipation of receiving insight that will deserve our later attention. We prepare ourselves for a spiritual feast no less dramatic than the wedding at Cana, when the Savior turned water into wine.

September 21

The Son of
our Great God
(Alma 24:13)

Latter-day Saints
ought to be more tolerant of
those who wear crosses as expressions
of their faith in **The Son of our Great God**.
After all, we have our own distinctive manner of
ornamentation and dress. We wear CTR rings and
Young Womanhood award medallions and Duty
to God pins, our young men are encouraged to
wear white shirts and ties, and our adult
members have adopted other unusual
articles of clothing that orient their
thoughts toward the covenants
they have made with
the Savior.

September 22

The Son of the Everlasting God
(1 Nephi 11:32)

No-one can dispute that a gathering is taking place. Israel again exists as a sovereign nation after almost 2,000 years as only a dream in the hearts of faithful Jews. Truly did **The Son of the Everlasting God** declare: "I will remember the covenant which I have made with my people that I would gather them together in mine own due time, that I would give unto them again the land of their fathers for their inheritance which is the promised land unto them forever." (3 Nephi 20:13).

September 23

The Son, the Only Begotten of the Father
(Alma 5:48)

There is a physical and a spiritual rapport between the Father and the Son, and between them and true believers. Through this connection, which is consumated by the Holy Ghost, we become "one" in the spiritual sense, with **The Son, the Only Begotten of the Father**.

September 24

Thou art my God
(Hosea 2:23)

When we are enthusiastic with religious fervor that results from divine inspiration, our exclamation **Thou art my God!** takes on a whole new meaning. Our best education is to be perpetually thrilled by life. Enthusiasm is a savory and pungent spice that adds both flavor and interest to everything into which it is blended.

September 25

Standard
(1 Nephi 21:22)

The most
important things our
Standard can provide for
us are the tools that will help
us to draw closer to our divine
center. If we fail to develop a
relationship with the Savior,
pivotal experiences that
could have been ours
will instead be
neutralized.

September 26

The Stone upon which they might Build and have Safe Foundation
(Jacob 4:15)

The Saints have been endowed with power by **The Stone upon which they might Build and have Safe Foundation**. The covenant of consecration, made at holy altars before God, angels, and witnesses, expedites our education, as we learn to temporally and spiritually govern ourselves and our families. This process of unification is consumated in the administration of sealing ordinances in the House of the Lord.

September 27

My
Support
(2 Nephi 4:20)

It is in the
temple that we receive
ordinances that round out our
mortal experience by portraying a
larger view of life. They smooth out the
rough edges that have been created as we bump
and grind our way through life. They put our trials
and tribulations in perspective, answer the questions that
have troubled our spirits, and enable us to comprehend the
mysteries of the kingdom with greater clarity. Participation
in ordinances answers questions we never thought to ask.
Church activity orients us toward the temple, permitting
us to see with the eye of faith. Temple ordinances that
are unambiguously performed provide a template
for a sum of experience that is greater than the
whole of any temporal education, and that
establishes a sure footing on Him
Who is **My Support**.

September 28

That God Who Brought the Children of Israel out of the Land of Egypt
(Mosiah 7:19)

Repetitively,
we need to be told to
repent because it is the hinge pin
upon which swings the door opening up
into the full expression of the Plan of Salvation.
When we feel, to even a small degree, the love and
gracious willingness on the part of **That God Who Brought
the Children of Israel out of the Land of Egypt** to suffer
for our sins, and we are led to repentance for all
of our transgressions, we feel our desire and
capacity to serve Him expanding within
us. We have been Born Again and we
are instilled with the vigor and
the innocence of childhood.

September 29

That God Who was the God of Abraham, and Isaac, and Jacob
(Mosiah 7:19)

The gathering of Israel in the Last Days is a preparation for her celestial destiny, a reunion with **That God Who was the God of Abraham, and Isaac, and Jacob**. "Graft in the branches," said the prophet Zenos. "Begin at the last that they may be first, and that the first may be last, and dig about the trees, both old and young, that all may be nourished once again for the last time."
(Jacob 5:63).

September 30

There is None other Name given under Heaven Save it be this Jesus Christ
(2 Nephi 25:20)

A rite
that has a present
spiritual meaning is a
symbol. No one would dispute
the symbolism of the ordinance of
baptism that is carried out in a font which
is in the similitude of the grave. In its waters
of purification, the repentant faithful symbolically
wash away their sins, and emerge clean in the sight
of God. Christ Himself was baptized in Jordan,
the lowest body of fresh water on the planet,
that enters the Dead Sea about 400 meters
below sea level. **There is None other
Name given under Heaven Save it
be this Jesus Christ**, to save us
from our sins. To do so, He
figuratively and literally
descended beneath
us all.

October 1

Thou art Angry, O Lord
(Alma 33:16)

**Thou art Angry,
O Lord,** when Thy chosen
people are puffed up in pride. In
the scriptures, we have been warned
repeatedly about this looming menace to our
temporal and spiritual welfare. The dirty time
bomb of pride is always ticking, threatening to
explode and scatter its lethal contents among
the disciples of Christ. Keeping pride in
check allows us to move beyond the
law of carnal commandments to
nobler principles that define
a celestial standard.

October 2

Thou
art God
(Alma 22:18)

Faith that
Thou art God
gives me the vision
to see beyond the limited
horizon of my natural eyes. The
Hubble telescope is so powerful that
if it were in New York City and could be
trained on Tokyo, Japan, it would be able to
distinguish between two objects that were as
little as ten feet apart. Faith is much more
powerful than that optical instrument.
With faith as a grain of mustard seed,
we are told that we could say to
a mountain, move, and it
would be done.

October 3

Thou art Merciful, O God
(Alma 33:4)

Because
Thou art Merciful,
O God, we resolve to
try harder, stand taller, walk
straighter, speak more gently, act
more responsibly, give more freely,
listen more attentively, think more
carefully, serve more faithfully,
receive more graciously, cry
more tenderly, and laugh
more heartily.

October 4

True and Faithful
(2 Nephi 31:15)

He Who is
True and Faithful
gently guides us to the first
principles of the Gospel. Then, as
our faith grows stronger, we experience a
bright recollection that snaps our sins into
sharp focus. Initially, our faith makes us
uncomfortable, uneasy, and unsettled.
But as we transition to repentance,
we experience the peace and the
assurance that leads us to the
waters of baptism and the
gift of the Holy
Ghost.

October 5

The True
and Living God
(1 Nephi 17:30)

When
we have been
in spiritual bondage,
but see in a sudden sunburst
of spiritual sensitivity that **The
True and Living God** is our Light,
it would be nice to entertain
sustaining support from a
sympathetic priesthood
to help us shed the
shackles of
sin.

October 6

The Lord
and His Goodness
(Hosea 3:5)

A regularly
recurring miracle that
we can witness on almost a daily
basis is not the raising of the physically
dead, but the healing of the spiritually sick.
Particularly in a temple setting, patrons can draw
upon the limitless reserves of **The Lord and His
Goodness**. His hand-picked trauma team,
with specialty training in advanced
spiritual life-support techniques,
stands ready to minister to
those in need.

October 7

The Very God of Israel
(1 Nephi 19:7)

When we are anxiously engaged, we have eliminated diversions and distractions, and give **The Very God of Israel** our undivided attention. We become immersed in worthwhile pursuits, are caught up in creative quests, and find ourselves engulfed in righteousness.

October 8

Our Great and Eternal Head
(Helaman 13:38)

When we make covenants,
we bind ourselves by our integrity
to act in certain ways. Covenants bring a
sense of responsibility, which in turn becomes
a reinforcement for positive action. Making covenants
with **Our Great and Eternal Head** can help us to break bad
habits, because the process orients us toward the course we
must pursue. We then establish a means of accountability
by making our obligation known to others. When we
make promises based on a correct understanding
of the consequences of our commitment, we
unify forces within ourselves to secure
the power and blessings
of heaven.

October 9

The Voice of the Lord
(3 Nephi 1:12)

All of us, at one time or another, feel the glimmering facets of the life of the spirit. We all believe in inspiration, or in **The Voice of the Lord**. Witness my Google search of the word "inspiration" that generated over 88 million results. The trick is getting people to believe that if we ask, it shall be given us, and if we seek, we shall find, and if we knock it shall be opened unto us. Should it be so surprising to us that Joseph Smith so spectacularly put the promise of James to the test?

October 10

The Power and Spirit of God, which was in Jesus Christ
(3 Nephi 7:21)

God is
sensitive to our
needs, and He hears
our prayers. In conformity
to eternal law, we may draw
upon the natural energy or life
force that we recognize as nothing
short of **The Power and Spirit of
God, which was in Jesus Christ**.
As we do so, we are, in effect,
touching His garment.

October 11

I am in the Father, and the Father in Me
(3 Nephi 9:15)

When
Jesus Christ
assured us: "**I am
in the Father, and the
Father in Me**," He revealed a
foundation principle of His Gospel.
Our confirmation of the validity of that
doctrine is composed of three ingredients.
First is our recognition of the principle. Second
is our familiarity with and understanding of
His teachings concerning the principle, and
third is our direct experience with the
principle, which we know to be
the fruits of faith.

October 12

With the Father from the Beginning
(3 Nephi 9:15)

Freedom
must not be confused
for the security afforded by
a prison cell, where armed guards
are at the ready to quell every disturbance
to the status quo, or mistaken for the sanctuary
of an intensive care unit, where life-support devices
are always available to countermand a D.N.R. order.
Life entails the assumption of risk, and our tendency to
look to others for financial security, social security, or job
security speaks for itself. It is the evidence of our desire
to avoid risk. He Who was **With the Father from the Beginning** has a much better way. He asks us to
take a special kind of a risk, to put our faith
and trust in Him, so that we might be
unencumbered by the long-term
negative consequences of
poor choices and yet be
free to reach our
potential.

October 13

The Lord God of Israel
was their Inheritance
(Joshua 13:33)

Faith
is an action
verb that leads us to
repentance. Zion is no
place for sinners, but there
is plenty of room for those
who have repented, who
seek **The Lord God of
Israel** Who is **their
Inheritance**.

October 14

I, and the
Holy Ghost are One
(3 Nephi 11:36)

There is
no revelation
where there is no
student, and as long as we
ask the wrong questions, we will
continue to be at odds with biblical faith
and will never bridge the gap between the
secular and the divine. "As humanity continues
to struggle with death, despair, hopelessness, fear,
and anxiety, the scriptures speak a far more relevant
message to society than any rational explanation."
("Newsweek," November 1980). Our recognition
of the implications of the Lord's declaration:
I, and the Holy Ghost are One, is itself
a revelatory experience that will
bring us closer to God.

October 15

One
(Doctrine & Covenants 50:43)

As we experience
the hard lessons of life that
are regularly thrown our way,
if we have not learned to follow the
example of forgiveness of the **One**, we
will become numb to the better angels of our
nature, and we will lose our capacity to touch
and to be touched by those around us. The
barriers we throw up will isolate us from
them, and we will become insulated
from the sensitivity that is critical
to our recognition of the steps
that must be taken in order
to activate the execution
of the Great Plan of
Happiness in our
behalf.

October 16

I am He
that Gave the Law
(3 Nephi 15:5)

Myths from around the world give the Milky Way its name and explain its origin. The Greeks believed it was created when suckling Heracles dribbled the breast milk of Hera, wife of Zeus, across the night sky. It was also described as the trail to Mount Olympus, the home of the Gods, and as the path of ruin made by the chariot of the Sun God Helios. In Sanskrit, the Milky Way was called Akash Ganga (Ganges of the Heavens), and was considered sacred. Hindu cosmology explains the galaxy as an ocean of milk churned by the gods for a thousand years in order to release Amrita, the nectar of immortal life. Christians have similar metaphysical beliefs; that it was **He that Gave the Law** Who created, not only the heavens, but also all that lies therein.

October 17

I am He Who Covenanted with My People Israel
(3 Nephi 15:5)

It is our temple worthiness that makes a Zion society possible. It allows the Saints to build up the Holy City wherever they are living in the world, and to commune with Him **Who Covenanted with** His **People Israel**. It allows Church members to make their homes places of purity, protection, love, and personal revelation.

October 18

My Rock
(3 Nephi 18:12)

As I strive in every way to live in
obedience to the laws and ordinances of the
Gospel of Jesus Christ that have been decreed
by **My Rock** to be necessary for exaltation, I will
prepare myself through sanctification by the spirit
to be led unerringly by the Lord. I may take Him at
His word when He says: "Mine angels shall go up
before you, and also my presence." (D&C 103:20).
I envision myself walking down a straight and
narrow path in the presence of God, angels,
and witnesses, past great and spacious
buildings, and through roiling mists
of darkness, all the way to the Tree
of Life, where I may bask in a
heavenly light that allows
me to see with clarity
as I partake of its
delicious
fruit.

October 19

I am the Light
which ye shall hold Up
(3 Nephi 18:24)

The
Savior
relied on our
universal familiarity
with light and darkness
when He said: **I am the Light
which ye shall hold Up**. He touched
upon chords of commonality and rooted
our faith when He explained: "Neither do
men light a candle, and put it under a
bushel, but on a candlestick; and it
giveth light unto all that are in
the house." (Matthew 5:15).

October 20

I am He of Whom Moses Spake
(3 Nephi 20:23)

Feeding
the flock of
**Him of Whom
Moses Spake** with
the nourishing Bread
of Life will eventually bring
the fold into harmony with the
attributes of the Good Shepherd.

October 21

The God of Israel Shall be your Rearward
(3 Nephi 20:42)

When you enjoy
the fruits of repentance,
you know that **The God of Israel
Shall be your Rearward**. He covers your
back, and makes it possible for your mind,
heart, and soul to experience the unspeakable
joy of forgiveness. His protective influence
offers you the promise of a platform for
personal progress, and a worthiness
foundation for the building
of a testimony of His
redeeming love.

October 22

Thy Maker, thy Husband,
the Lord of Hosts is His Name
(3 Nephi 22:5)

The looming tragedy is not what may happen to our society, but what we have already done to ourselves. Our **Maker**, our **Husband, the Lord of Hosts is His Name** has admonished us to hold our ground. "Stand in the office which I have appointed unto you," He said. "Succor the weak, lift up the hands which hang down, and strengthen the feeble knees." (D&C 81:5). In the world, there is a flight from that quality of compassion, and of connection with others. Ours is the age of the half-done job, of mediocre effort, and of passing the buck. Citizenship in the kingdom requires a higher standard and correspondingly greater effort. His disciples light candles, rather than curse the darkness. If damage has already been done, it does not need to be irreversible.

October 23

The Lord that hath Mercy on Thee
(3 Nephi 22:10)

Magnifying your calling means to build it up in dignity and importance, to make it honorable and commendable in the eyes of others, to enlarge and strengthen it; simply, to "perform the service that pertains to it." (Joseph Smith). "If you do not magnify your calling," **The Lord that hath Mercy on Thee** will "hold you responsible for those you might have saved, had you done your duty."
(John Taylor).

October 24

I will be a Swift Witness
(3 Nephi 24:5)

The Lord said: **I will be a Swift Witness,** and to that end we seek the companionship of the Holy Ghost. We allow Him to illuminate our minds with the answers to our questions. We take a pause in our busy schedules to think about the weightier matters of the law. We let our minds work on the application of Gospel principles to our daily experiences, always remembering to listen for the Still Small Voice.

October 25

The Son of Righteousness
(3 Nephi 25:2)

We bear
adversity well when
we follow the stellar example of
The Son of Righteousness. Hardship
often proves to be a springboard to later success,
and looming problems often disguise solutions that
are just around the corner. In fact, the Chinese word for
danger is composed of two characters that represent
"crisis" and "opportunity." Once we have received
the anointing of courage that attends the faithful,
we "can never rest until the last enemy is
conquered, death is destroyed, and
truth reigns triumphant."
(Parley P. Pratt).

October 26

Christ, Who was before the World Began
(3 Nephi 26:5)

We must be familiar with
the vital issues of the day, and
be ready to stand up and strengthen
family values. Then we must move out
of our comfort zones into our communities
and countries, in order to stem an advancing
tide that threatens to erode the foundations of
the pillars of society. For generations, these
supports have remained in place to secure
our future. **Christ, Who was before the
World Began**, enjoys a longitudinal
perspective on this principle, and
knows that a thousand points
of light, taken together, cast
a very long shadow.

October 27

Christ
for their Shepherd
(Mormon 5:17)

The gift of eternal life is not
thrust upon those who are unprepared or
unacquainted with **Christ for their Shepherd**,
or forced upon those who are unwilling to make a
sacrifice today to secure a blessing tomorrow. Mortality
has been designed as a life-long work project to give
all of us enough time to mold our nature to more
closely resemble that of God. When He has
perfected us, we will be caught up to the
third heaven, as was Paul. Then, as
we kneel before our Father at
His throne, He will see in
us a reflection of both
His image and His
likeness.

October 28

The Very Christ and the Very God
(Mormon 3:21)

When we have received the image of **The Very Christ and the Very God** in our countenances, our faces will reflect His light. As we experience this mighty change in our hearts, we will be Born Again. The world seeks to manipulate us from the outside, and fails miserably. But the Gospel transforms us from the inside, and succeeds brilliantly. Thus, we are created to reach our potential that is reflected, not only in the image of God, but also in His likeness.

October 29

The Eternal Father of Heaven
(Mormon 6:22)

Those
who demand
overt evidence of the
awesome power of **The
Eternal Father of Heaven**
as a condition for belief seek
to circumvent the process by
which faith is developed. They
want proof without paying the
price. Like adulterers, they seek
results but are unwilling to accept
the corresponding responsibilities.
Their obsessive and compulsive
focus of attention is fixed on
the influential aphrodesiac
of a perverted theological
titillation.

October 30

Jesus Christ, even the Father and the Son
(Mormon 9:12)

The attrition of
our civil and religious
liberties cannot be summarily
eliminated, and so we must initiate
damage control protocols and effective
countermeasures as quickly as possible to
try to contain assaults on our basic freedoms.
Jesus Christ, even the Father and the Son, gently
reminds us that it is easier to hold up an umbrella
than it is to turn off the rain. At the same time,
let us not forget that "vice is a monster of so
frightful mien, as to be hated needs but
to be seen. Yet seen too oft, familiar
with her face, we first endure,
then pity, then embrace."
(Alexander Pope).

October 31

The Holiness
of Jesus Christ
(Mormon 9:5)

A
powerful
expression of the
culmination of the process of
repentance is the ordinance of the
Sacrament. However, we do not partake
of the emblems of bread and water in order
to obtain a remission of our sins, but rather to
recommit ourselves to our baptismal covenants,
and to receive **The Holiness of Jesus Christ**,
so that we might shun sinful behavior in
the future as we more securely hold
fast to the Rod of Iron.

November 1

An Unchangeable Being
(Mormon 9:19)

When government usurps powers to siphon off the productivity of its citizens, when it stifles creativity, or when taxpayers give involuntarily for the support of entitlement programs from which they receive no benefit, the chains of slavery tighten around them. From **An Unchangeable Being**, we learn that when rulers are supported in their laziness and idolatry, it is all too easy for the people to adopt their wicked ways, as they are deceived and led astray by vain and flattering words.

November 2

Almighty Power
(Mormon 9:26)

Marriage is the
noblest manifestation
of the connection that can exist
between a man and a woman, and is
the expression of a covenant relationship
that will help them to more clearly visualize
their divine nature and conjoined future. In fact,
matrimony is one of the seven holy sacraments
of the Catholic Church, and is a doctrine upon
which Latter-day Saints agree. We believe
that the institution of marriage lies at
the foundation of the experiences
the **Almighty Power** has
conceived for His
children.

November 3

God of our Salvation
(Psalms 65:5)

Latter-day Saints believe that our covenants reveal the parenting style of the **God of our Salvation**. Covenants help us, more than any other thing, to focus our efforts to become as He is. The Saints go to great effort to make covenants with God, because they believe that these special promises are integral to the Plan and make it possible for them to realize their dream to become as their Father is. They view covenants as powerful teaching tools that reveal His amazing attributes.

November 4

The Father of the Heavens and of the Earth, and all Things that in Them Are
(Ether 4:7)

The Father of the Heavens and of the Earth, and all Things that in Them Are gives certain principles for us to follow, and by obedience, blessings and power freely flow. But we have no proof of His promises until we act on the basis of faith, trust, and belief. Then comes a quiet confirmation of His assurances. That is why the scriptures teach: "Faith, if it hath not works, is dead, being alone." (James 2:17).

November 5

I am He Who Speaketh
(Ether 4:8)

The natural inclination of those who have found the truth is to share it with others. The Savior saw the big picture. He wasn't constrained by perceived limitations, but urged His disciples: "Go ye into all the world, and preach the gospel to every creature," for **I am He Who Speaketh**. "
(Mark 16:15).

November 6

I am the Father
(Ether 4:12)

By the
power of the Spirit, the
Savior reveals to the righteous,
I am the Father, but the testimony of
His divinity is withheld from the unworthy.
Perhaps His P.I.N. is carefully guarded simply
because the undeserved knowledge of His
existence is the ultimate form of identity
theft. It could be that He simply wants
to control invasive harassment by
the paparazzi, as well as the
voracious feeding frenzy
of exploitation upon
which our tabloids
depend.

November 7

I am the Same that Leadeth Men to all Good
(Ether 4:12)

Our Savior is **the Same that Leadeth Men to all Good.** If, during that journey, we are off course by even one degree, it may be small enough, at least initially, to escape our attention. But it is not insignificant. Without our conscious correction, even a tiny deviation from a dead-on orientation toward our great Example can have devastating long-term consequences.

November 8

The Truth
of the World
(Ether 4:9)

Temple patrons shall "grow like a cedar in Lebanon. Those that be planted in the house of the Lord shall flourish in the courts of our God." (Psalms 92:12-13). To those unfamiliar with travel in harsh environments, palms often seem to grow in desert wastes. It is only upon closer inspection that they notice the oases of underlying currents of life-sustaining water that bring nourishment to the roots of the thirsty trees. So too, **The Truth of the Word** provides sustenance to those who come to His house, hungering and thirsting for divine guidance.

November 9

It is I that hath Spoken It
(Ether 4:19)

When we receive personal revelation, we recognize from Whom it comes, that **It is I that hath Spoken It**. In the House of the Lord, we enjoy an unpolluted atmosphere with a clarity that allows us to see things as they really are, so that we can make choices based on sureties, rather than on speculation or the vagaries of men. We catch a glimpse of eternity as we brush against the veil, almost rubbing shouders with those on the other side.

November 10

The Gift
of His Son
(Ether 12:11)

Those
who establish
covenants with God
realize that **The Gift of His
Son** is priceless. They would never
mock Him by breaking their part of the
bargain they have made with Him. There
is an unalterable cause and effect relationship
that is associated with the commandments.
The Law of the Harvest dictates results
that are consistent with the quality
of our performance.

November 11

A More Excellent Way
(Ether 12:11)

In our society, we no longer put to death those who violate the Law of the Sabbath. We have **A More Excellent Way**. And yet, we die spiritually and thwart the purpose of the Plan of Salvation when we deliberately alienate ourselves from His influence, because we have put a hold on our steady progress toward an eternal destiny.

November 12

The Finisher of their Faith
(Moroni 6:4)

The Finisher of their Faith is the tangible expression of a type, which is a symbol that points to a future reality. Israel had the Brazen Serpent and the Nephites had the Liahona. We have the sacrament and the endowment in the temple. In the tokens of His body and His blood, and in the House of the Lord, we discover the elements of a celestial compass that provides the bearings on eternity that must be followed if we are to orient ourselves toward the light of His glorious kingdom.

November 13

His
Holy Will
(Moroni 7:2)

We are
one body
in Christ, and
are obedient to **His
Holy Will** and the wise
counsel of His prophet. We
make sure that new members
of the Lord's Church have a
friend, opportunities for
service, and that they
are nourished by
the good word
of God.

November 14

Jesus is the Christ
(Moroni 7:44)

The Lord has given us the Word of Wisdom as a litmus test of our faith and testimony. It is a barometer that can tangibly measure how we are handling the stewardship of our mortal clay. Our bodies operate in harmony with the spirit to make up our souls. Therefore, since they will be everlastingly joined with our spirits on the other side of the veil, they must be kept pure and holy through all the trials of mortality. We fill the measure of our creation only when we are true to its purpose. That means we must be prepared to present ourselves at the pleasing bar of God in outstanding physical and stellar spiritual condition, ready to declare that **Jesus is the Christ**. It naturally follows that to use our bodies, or our minds for that matter, for purposes for which they were not created, frustrates the execution of the Plan.

November 15

His Son, Jesus Christ
(Moroni 7:48)

The Book of Psalms praises God, and bears a powerful witness of the mission of **His Son, Jesus Christ**. Its beautiful poetical language also reminds us of the great blessings that we have been given, and it suggests ways for us to express gratitude for our many gifts and favors.

November 16

He
is Pure
(Moroni 7:48)

"No more sacred word exists in secular or holy writ than that of mother." (Ezra Taft Benson). This seems like a particularly bold statement, especially in light of some other powerful words that come to mind, like Savior, Celestial Kingdom, Atonement, Repentance, Forgiveness, and so on. But "mother" is the keystone of the Gospel arch, and is central to the Plan of Salvation. **He is Pure**, and without His mother, and ours for that matter, there would be no-one to participate in the Plan.

November 17

His Holy Child, Jesus
(Moroni 8:3)

If, instead of God, we choose rationalization, mediocrity, selfish pleasures, the things of the world, the honors of men, or willful disobedience, our priorities are out of order, and we will disappoint **His Holy Child, Jesus**. As long as we remain in this state, we can never partake of the fruit of the Tree of Life. The world before us will be as a barren desert, littered with telestial trash, devoid of refreshing oases, the welcome shade of trees, and the abundance of well-watered and fruited gardens.

November 18

He is Unchangeable from all Eternity to all Eternity
(Moroni 8:18)

The
mind of God
can be known, because
**He is Unchangeable from all
Eternity to all Eternity**. His mysteries
are quite simply the saving principles of
the Gospel that are received with the eye of
faith, by personal revelation. When we have
spiritually prepared ourselves to internalize
the testimony of a Gospel principle, the
mysteries of God are unfolded to our
view, and we are one step further
along the pathway defined by
a Rod of Iron, that leads
to eternal life.

November 19

Our Lord Jesus Christ, Who Sitteth on the Right Hand of His Power
(Moroni 9:26)

When we accept as our Master **Our Lord Jesus Christ, Who Sitteth on the Right Hand of His Power**, our testimonies are charged with energy, and we link our feelings with those of the two disciples on the Road to Emmaus, who, after communing with the resurrected Lord, declared: "Did not our hearts burn within us, while he talked with us by the way?" (Luke 24:32).

November 20

A
Voice
(3 Nephi 9:1)

As we mature
in the Gospel, we become
sensitized to **A Voice** that speaks
within our souls, urging us on to noble
effort. When we have fought a good fight,
and the time comes for each of us to confidently
give our report, the Lord will eagerly take us to His
bosom and declare: "Well done, thou good and faithful
servant. Thou hast been faithful over a few things.
I will make thee ruler over many things. Enter
thou into the joy of thy lord."
(Matthew 25:21).

November 21

The
Founder of Peace
(Mosiah 15:18)

"Men's and nations' finest hours are those when extraordinary challenge is met with extraordinary response." (Winston Churchill). Our courage to face demagogues can be the catalyst that transforms our timidity and temerity into powerful presence of mind, which then acts as a platform for assertive action. It is not bravado, but boldness. It is not a paper tiger, but is an intense and compellingly positive response to threat. In the fight or flight scenario, it is the launch pad for the anticipated adrenalin rush that carries us beyond the challenge directly to **The Founder of Peace** Himself.

November 22

The Only Wise and True God, and Jesus Christ, Whom He hath Sent
(Doctrine & Covenants 132:24)

We sometimes forget that it is not the Apostasy that is evidence of the Restoration. Rather, it is the other way around: It is the Restoration that is evidence of the Apostasy. Because we believe that a Restoration is taking place, it follows that we affirm that there was an Apostasy that was foretold by **The Only Wise and True God, and Jesus Christ, Whom He hath Sent**.

November 23

Received the Fulness of the Father
(Doctrine & Covenants 76:71)

Those of us who have had a spiritual heart transplant, who have **Received the Fulness of the Father**, must take "anti-rejection medication" for the rest of our lives. In addition, after the operation comes physically and spiritually challenging rehab therapy. We must pay attention to what we ingest, avoiding certain foods and activities. We must conduct our lives in moderate and temperate ways, and also participate in regular and consistent spiritually aerobic exercise in order to strengthen our new heart and avoid jeopardizing our new-found health.

November 24

The Same Unchangeable God
(Doctrine & Covenants 20:17)

In contrast to **The Same Unchangeable God** Whom we worship as we sit on His right hand, the telestial turf of secular humanism is Satan's home ground. If we venture onto it, we risk losing our way. The quicksand of a misleading, left-leaning, liberal ideology that accepts everything and risks nothing lies ready to suck the unwary into the underworld of the adversary.

November 25

Son Ahman; or, in other words, Alphus
(Doctrine & Covenants 95:17)

In order to shed light on the solemnities of eternity, it is necessary to believe all that **Son Ahman; or, in other words, Alphus** has revealed, all that He does now reveal, and to have the faith that He will continue to reveal many great and important things pertaining to the Kingdom. Without the knowledge gained through modern revelation, we risk the fate foreseen by Isaiah, who prophesied that, in the Last Days, the simple messages of the Gospel would be needlessly complicated by confusing ecclesiastical embroidery. "The earth also is defiled under the inhabitants thereof, because they have transgressed the laws, changed the ordinance, and broken the everlasting covenant." (Isaiah 24:5).

November 26

I am the True Light that Lighteth every Man that Cometh into the World
(Doctrine & Covenants 93:2)

Our place in
the cosmos is molded
by our interaction with **The
True Light that Lighteth every
Man that Cometh into the World**. Esau
evidently didn't have a good grasp of that fact.
He sold his birthright for a mess of pottage,
evoking an image that suggests far more
than the loss of his next meal. In
fact, he profaned a very special
relationship and lost his
identity as a chosen
vessel of God.

November 27

I am with the Faithful Always
(Doctrine & Covenants 62:9)

The Savior is **with the Faithful Always.** If we do not choose Him, but instead demean our potential for true greatness by settling for mediocrity, if we rationalize our weaknesses, succumb to our desire to be temporally titillated by selfish pleasures or the things of the world, if we seek the honors of men that are handed out like candy on Halloween from the doorways and windows of great and spacious buildings, or if we are willfully disobedient to His commandments, our priorities are out of order. As long as we remain in this state, we will never partake of the fruit of the Tree of Life.

November 28

Your Father which is in Heaven
(Doctrine & Covenants 84:92)

The
best approach to
come to a knowledge of
our **Father which is in Heaven**
is to love Him through lowliness
of heart, humility, and meekness,
which describe an attitude that
is the product of voluntary
effort rather than the
result of external
constraints.

November 29

I am He Who said Other Sheep have I Which are not of this Fold
(Doctrine & Covenants 10:59)

Latter-day Saints believe the Lord when He says: **I am He Who said Other Sheep have I Which are not of this Fold**. He taught: "Because that ye have a Bible ye need not suppose that it contains all my words; neither need ye suppose that I have not caused more to be written." (2 Nephi 29:10). There are important reasons why there must be more scripture than that which has been provided in the Bible. One of these is that His concern is not only for the Jews, but also for all nations under heaven.

November 30

From Everlasting to Everlasting
(Doctrine & Covenants 20:17)

If we accept the doctrine that there was an apostasy, we might ask: "What were its causes? Did it take God, Who is **From Everlasting to Everlasting**, by surprise, or does it fit into the overall implementation of the Plan? Does the Plan make allowances for those who lived through the long night of darkness? Did the Apostasy inflict eternally damaging consequences on those who endured it, or could it have provided a shield of protection in some way? How are those living in the Last Days positively influenced by the events that occurred before the Restoration of truth?

December 1

God
is Merciful
(Doctrine & Covenants 2:10)

In the Last Days,
as the Restoration gains
momentum, we are assaulted on
many fronts by those who do not believe
as we do, whose self-anointed mission is to
tear down the faith and testimony of others. If
we pause at forks in the road in order to explore
tempting detours from the straight and narrow path,
or to get our tickets punched by every uninformed
skeptic and nattering nabob of negativism with a
personal agenda to promote, we risk weakening
our faith in the foundation principles that are
our protection, by alienating ourselves from
our **God** Who **is Merciful**. Curiosity only
killed the cat because it didn't know
how to direct its attention to
worthwhile areas
of inquiry.

December 2

I am He Who Spake in Righteousness
(Doctrine & Covenants 133:47)

When we listen
to the counsel of Him **Who
Spake in Righteousness**, our lives
embrace a contagious vibrancy. As our
knowledge increases, so do our responsibility
and commitment to obedience. As our testimonies
of Christ swell, faith intensifies our desire to repent. In
this sense, when our lives are in harmony with Gospel
principles, we are in a constant state of improvement
leading to perfection. Becoming Christ-like is the
ultimate, incredible journey. It is the road less
traveled, but even the visualization of our
destination gives our experiences along
the way a sense of meaning
and purpose.

December 3

Him Who has Ordained you from on High
(Doctrine & Covenants 77:2)

Whatever your perceived inadequacies, you have this great truth upon which you can rely: You have been empowered by **Him Who has Ordained you from on High**. Beethoven composed some of his finest music after he had become deaf. Demosthenes overcame a speech impediment to become one of the greatest orators of Classical Greece. Early in his career, Abraham Lincoln said: "I will prepare myself, and some day my chance will come."

December 4

I am He
Who was Slain
(Doctrine & Covenants 110:4)

When
we pause
to consider the
mortal ministry of
He Who was Slain, we
have a renewed passion to
press forward with complete
dedication. Our sole desire is to
feast upon the word of Christ and
to receive physical and spiritual
nourishment and strength, so
that we might endure to the
end with responsibility
and accountability.

December 5

I, the Lord, am Merciful
(Doctrine & Covenants 70:18)

The Lord
is **Merciful**, which is
especially good news to those
of us who have not yet developed the
discipline to control our cravings. With every
gift of power is attached the temptation to abuse it,
and unbridled freedom to indulge in every whim can
lead to a very real tyranny. Of that class of individuals,
Edmund Burke said: "Their passions forge their fetters."
Recognition of our unseemly behavior, with remorse for
having let the Lord down, making restitution whenever
possible, reforming our conduct and refraining from
repeating it, relating to the Lord's mercy in our
behalf, and realizing that we have received
His forgiveness, are the necessary steps
in breaking free from the shackes
of sin and the tyranny
of the tempter.

December 6

I am the Life and the Light of the World
(Doctrine & Covenants 11:28)

When we back
others into a corner,
the only way they can
come out is fighting. But
when we illuminate their
options with **the Life and
the Light of the World**,
they are instilled with
a sense of direction
and purpose that
shines in their
eyes.

December 7

A Light which Cannot be Hid in Darkness
(Doctrine & Cvoenants 14:9)

Our faith in Jesus Christ can be a spiritual strong searchlight allowing us to fearlessly take a few steps into the gloom of uncertainty. Only then, **A Light which Cannot be Hid in Darkness** will illuminate the path that lies ahead.

December 8

Like
Fuller's Soap
(Doctrine & Covenants 128:24)

**Like
Fuller's Soap** that
was used anciently to
clean and whiten clothing,
Jesus came to the earth to
purify us by washing
away the stain
of sin.

December 9

The Lord God,
the Mighty One of Israel
(Doctrine & Covenants 36:1)

When we are
zealous, we attend to our
duties and our responsibilities
with ardent feeling and with fervor.
We enthusiastically support **The Lord God,
the Mighty One of Israel**, and we feel His power.
If we allow ourselves to be overzealous, however, we
shoot the arrow blindly, and then move the target so that
we can score what we mistakenly think is a bulls-eye. If
we distort the doctrine or wrest the scriptures in our
defense of truth, or if fanaticism deforms our core
values, we will strain our eyes as we lose our
focus, and we will look beyond the mark.
What could have been our finest hour
will slip between our fingers as we
lose our sense of touch.

December 10

The Lord is God, and
beside Him there is no Savior
(Doctrine & Covenants 76:1)

As we face
our challenges, we remind
ourselves that **The Lord is God,
and beside Him there is no Savior**. It is
He Who gives us the courage to continue our
struggle, and to be less concerned about winning or
losing individual battles. He knows that it is the outcome
that matters most, and so He wants us to win the war. What
is important to Him is that we carry on after each defeat. In
our relentless pursuit of excellence, we will face our fair
share of trials, tailored to meet our individual needs.
These are not stumbling blocks to our progression,
but are instead stepping stones that have been
designed by our Creator to take us to greater
heights of achievement. The struggle will
continue for as long as need be, and so
we must rely on Him to sustain us
over the long haul, particularly
when we feel that we have
reached the limits of
our endurance.

December 11

The Lord your God, even Jesus Christ, your
Advocate, Who Knoweth the Weakness of Man
and how to Succor them who are Tempted
(Doctrine & Covenants 62:1)

When
you know that
**The Lord is your God,
even Jesus Christ, your Advocate,
Who Knoweth the Weakness of Man
and how to Succor them who are Tempted**,
good outweighs evil, love overpowers jealousy,
hate, and prejudice, light drives out darkness, humility
displaces pride, knowledge banishes ignorance, courtesy
overwhelms rudeness, simplicity overshadows perplexity,
appreciation overcomes thanklessness, well-being replaces
weakness, abundance supersedes poverty, faith subdues
fear, joy deposes unhappiness, sadness, dejection, and
misery, harmony supplants discord, confidence is
substituted for timidity, hope casts out despair,
charity ousts selfishness, certainty dethrones
bewilderment, and assurance addresses
our discouragement.

December 12

He is a Man like Ourselves
(Doctrine & Covenants 129:1)

Nearly all of us will have temporal and spiritual challenges with which to deal, but chastisement is something special. It is a personalized invitation from the Lord to repent. **He is a Man like Ourselves**, and so we remember His example during the trials that are placed before us. We strengthen our testimonies through fasting and prayer, as we prepare ourselves each week to receive the Sacrament. In the scriptures, we study the illustrations of Gospel principles in order to deepen our understanding of their application. We make the sweet spirit within the temple a regular part of our religious experience. We avoid compromising situations and their trigger points, and we wisely exercise our agency to resist temptation. We act upon our spiritual promptings.

December 13

A Refiner and Purifier of Silver
(Doctrine & Covenants 128:24)

A 140 pound
human being is made
up of roughly 10 trillion cells.
Each cell is composed of 20 billion
protein molecules. Each protein molecule
has, on average, 14,000 atoms. Each atom has
up to 49 matter particles consisting of the nucleus,
protons, electrons, etc.. Each of those matter particles
is composed of roughly one million photons, the basic
unit of electro-magnetic energy. Fundamentally, we
are beings of light who radiate with the power of
Him Who is **A Refiner and Purifier of Silver**.
When He looks at us, He sees our potential,
manifest as trillions upon trillions of
individual glowing points whose
combined brilliance is enough
to illuminate even the
farthest reaches
of eternity.

December 14

The Voice of
the Day of the Lord
(Zephaniah 1:14)

We listen to **The Voice of the Day of the Lord** by reading uplifting literature and by exercising our minds and our spirits with stimulating thoughts, beautiful music, and meaningful conversation with others. We speak with purpose, and maintain a working knowledge of the current events that shape the world around us, but we ignore the media when it focuses its attention on talking heads or telestial trivia. We push ourselves to develop new interests, and are mentors to those who show promise in areas in which we have learned to excel.

December 15

The Same which Came in the Meridian of Time unto Mine Own, and Mine Own Received me Not
(Doctrine & Covenants 39:3)

The Same which Came in the Meridian of Time unto Mine Own, and Mine Own Received me Not, was to be their "Advocate," a term used just once in the New Testament. "If any man sin, and repent," taught the Savior, "we have an advocate with the Father, Jesus Christ the righteous," for He "is the propitiation for our sins, and not for ours only, but also for the sins of the whole world."
(1 John 1-2).

December 16

The Same which Knoweth all Things, for all Things are Present before Mine Eyes
(Doctrine & Covenants 38:2)

When we take into
consideration the fact that Christ is
**The Same which Knoweth all Things,
for all Things are Present before (His) Eyes**,
we approach Gospel scholarship differently. For
once, our study is not a race. No longer do we have
to finish a prescribed number of pages of scripture each
day. We spend several days with a single chapter or verse.
We read topically if we want to. We pause to discover what
other prophets have written about the same subjects. As we
memorize passages, we try to understand them in context
with the overall message. The word of God blooms with
hidden meaning we hadn't been aware of, and from
time to time its relevancy pops into our minds
just when we need it the most.

December 17

He was the Word, even the Messenger of Salvation
(Doctrine & Covenants 93:8)

We believe that Jesus Christ **was the Word, even the Messenger of Salvation**, and that the value of His gifts to us is incalculable. And so, we cultivate our gratitude, because we realize that its omission is a sin even greater than revenge. With revenge, we return evil for evil, but with ingratitude, we return evil for good. Even thankfulness may not be enough, because it consists only of words. But gratitude is the completion of thanks, and is shown by our actions.

December 18

Your Father,
Who is in Heaven
(Doctrine & Covenants 84:83)

You have
many of the noble
characteristics of **Your
Father, Who is in Heaven**, that
require the softening influence of your
love before they can become divine qualities.
Love allows you to bridge the gulf between the
world of everyday, and the land unpromised and
unearned. God, Who is the personification of every
good grace, is the embodiment of the heavenly
aether of love that allows you to see through
His eyes, so that you may catch a fleeting
glimpse of eternity and sample
the scented fragrance of its
celestial air.

December 19

Alpha and Omega, your Lord and your God
(Doctrine & Covenants 75:1)

On a grand scale,
we maintain our focus by
using symbols to answer the questions
of where we came from, why we are here, and
where we are going. Our divine potential is defined
by the Plan of Salvation, the Plan of Redemption, or the
Plan of Happiness, all centered on the Atonement of
Jesus Christ, Who is **Alpha and Omega, your
Lord and your God**. This takes us back
to the being of God Himself, whom
we simply call "Father."

December 20

The Framer of Heaven and Earth,
and all Things which are in Them
(Doctrine & Coenants 20:17)

**The Framer
of Heaven and Earth,
and all Things which are in
Them** uses the teachings and rituals of
the temple to take us on an upward journey
toward eternal life, ending with our symbolical
introduction into the presence of God. The characters
depicted, the physical setting, the clothing worn, and the
signs given in the temple are designed to help us to
recognize and expand upon our appreciation of
truth and to secure our commitment to be
obedient to our covenants. Therein lies
the source of our power to mature
into a spiritual interdependence
with each other and with
our Heavenly Father.

December 21

Him Who Sitteth upon the Throne, even the Lamb
(Doctrine & Covenants 88:115)

Within the walls of the temple, **Him Who Sitteth upon the Throne, even the Lamb**, teaches us principles that enable us to become purified so that we may be worthy to live once again in a state of holiness in His kingdom. Our spiritual renewal teaches us how to pass by angels who stand as sentinels, and to approach the veil, prepared to enter the presence of the Lord. But first, we must submit to His will, yield our hearts to Him, and live in harmony with all of the teachings of His Gospel. We trust in the Lord's assurance: "If ye do these things, blessed are ye, for ye shall be lifted up at the last day."
(3 Nephi 27:22).

December 22

Alpha and Omega, even Jesus Christ
(Doctrine & Covenants 81:7)

The song of the heart may be inaudible, but its intuitive melody can brighten our day and lighten our burdens just as effectively as would a choir of angels. As Hugh B. Brown said: "Sometimes during solitude I hear truth spoken with clarity and freshness; uncolored and untranslated it speaks from within myself in a language original but inarticulate, heard only with the soul." When filled with gratitude for **Alpha and Omega, even Jesus Christ**, our hearts burst into song as did the heavenly host that attended His birth.

December 23

A Light which Shineth in Darkness and the Darkness Comprehendeth it Not
(Doctrine & Covenants 39:2)

When we
open our scriptures to
the book of Luke, and we carefully
unwrap our Nativity scenes to gently place
the carvings of Joseph, Mary, and the baby Jesus
in the mangers that are prominently displayed in our
homes, the Spirit confirms **A Light which Shineth
in Darkness and the Darkness Comprehendeth
it Not**. We contemplate His gifts of peace on
earth and good will toward all men. The
birth of our Lord is an intensely
personal Christmas miracle
that was meant to be
shared with the
world.

December 24

The Marvelous Light of God
(Mosiah 27:29)

To the Nephites, on the eve of the mortal birth of **The Marvelous Light of God** there was given a sign, for at the going down of the sun on what turned out to be Christmas Eve, the people were astonished because there was no darkness. Instead, their world was filled with the light of Christ, "the light which is in all things, which giveth life to all things, which is the law by which all things are governed, even the power of God, who sitteth upon his throne, who is in the bosom of eternity, who is in the midst of all things." (D&C 88:13).

How appropriate that the sign of the birth of the Savior should be the dissolution of the night.

December 25

A Light
to the Gentiles
(1 Nephi 21:6)

None of us
were actually there
to hear the prophets and
the angels testify of His birth.
We did not see with our eyes the
new star that appeared in the East, nor
did we hear with our ears the heavenly host
praising God. We were not dazzled by **A Light
to the Gentiles** that pierced the darkness throughout
the night before His birth. We know that as He grew to
manhood "he spake not as other men, neither could he
be taught; for he needed not that any man should teach
him." (J.S.T. Matthew 3:25). But none of us were first
hand witnesses of these things. Nevertheless, even
after the story has been repeated for over 2,000
years, His power is such that it can reach
across the ages to touch us just as if we
had been present when the gift of
that first Christmas was
unwrapped.

December 26

Perfect
(3 Nephi 12:48)

The
U.S. Postal Service
dead-letter department
receives tens of thousands
of letters from children that
are addressed to Santa Claus,
asking for toys. How many
letters, do you think, are
sent after the holidays,
thanking him for
the **Perfect**
gift?

December 27

A
Child
(2 Nephi 19:6)

If the scriptures
have become so twisted that
they are no longer the sweet witness
for the Christ **Child** that they were meant
to be, and if the intent, meaning, and execution
of the ordinances of salvation have been so distorted
that they are meaninglesss and incomprehensible, it is
an abomination, because those caught in the snares
of misunderstanding and false doctrine jeopardize
their progression. For those who find themselves
in these circumstances, the very purpose of
mortality in the great Plan of Salvation
will have been compromised.

December 28

Eternal King
(Doctrine & Covenants 128:23)

Ours is a
holy society, and a
tight-knit community
of true believers. How
reassuring to know
that the One Who
stands at our
head is our
**Eternal
King**.

December 29

A
Sacrifice for Sin
(2 Nephi 2:7)

The gloomy opacity of doubt can obscure the true vision of our hearts, but He Who made **A Sacrifice for Sin** will replace our fear with saving faith.

December 30

That Great High Priest, that is Passed into the Heavens
(Hebrews 4:14)

**That Great High Priest,
that is Passed into the Heavens**
calls the earth His footstool. We leave
to His better judgment the bestowal of its
treasures, and focus instead, on the riches of
eternity. Too often, though, the love of money
captures our attention, clutching us in its strong
grip. In a fierce competition with the better angels
of our nature, we are left with soul scars and with
character stains that cannot be removed with
dry cleaning alone. It is necessary for us to
consumate the process of repentance by
immersing ourselves completely
in the healing waters
of baptism.

December 31

He is the Same, and His Years never Fail
(Doctrine & Covenants 76:4)

He is the Same, and His Years never Fail. He is bound by guidelines just as we are, and the world can be defined by its opposites as well as by itself. The appearance of the adversary in the Garden will attest to that fact.

The End

Minute Musings

Spontaneous Combustions of Thought

Volume Two

Appendix One

A Chronological List of
366 Scriptural References to Jesus Christ

"That which cometh from above is sacred, and must be
spoken with care, and by constraint of the Spirit."
(Doctrine & Covenants 63:64).

compiled by

Philip M. Hudson

January

1. The Lord, even the Savior (Doctrine & Covenants 133:25)
2. The Shadow of Thing to Come (Colossians 2:17)
3. Jesus, the Mediator of the New Covenant (Doctrine & Covenants 107:19)
4. The Lord Jesus Christ, the Son of the Father (2 Nephi 11:32)
5. God the Eternal Father (Doctrine & Covenants 20:77)
6. The Messenger of Salvation (Doctrine & Covenants 93:8)
7. The Christ, the Eternal God (2 Nephi 26:12)
8. Man of Holiness is My Name (Moses 7:35)
9. A God of Glory (Moses 1:20)
10. The Rock That is Higher Than I (Psalms 62:1)
11. Stem of Jesse (Isaiah 11:1)
12. A Prophet (Deuteronomy 18:15)
13. The Great Mediator (2 Nephi 2:28)
14. A Figure for the Time then Present (Hebrews 9:9)
15. A Rock of Offense to Both the Houses of Israel (Isaiah 8:14)
16. A Stumbling Stone and Rock of Offense (Romans 9:33)
17. Messiah, the King of Zion, the Rock of Heaven (Moses 7:53)
18. I, God (Doctrine & Covenants 19:16)
19. I am God (Moses 7:35)
20. Christ the Power of God and the Wisdom of God (1 Corinthians 1:24)
21. The Only Begotten (Moses 3:18)
22. Jesus is the Very Christ (2 Nephi 26:12)
23. I, The Lord God (Moses 3:6)
24. Only Begotten, even Jesus Christ (Moses 7:50)
25. The Righteous (Moses 7:47)
26. The Lord thy God (Abraham 2:7)
27. Him that hath Called us to Glory and Virtue (2 Peter 1:3)
28. A God of Gods (Deuteronomy 10:17)
29. God in the Highest (Luke 2:14)
30. My God, and your God (Moses 6:43)
31. A Prince and a Savior (Acts 5:31)

February

1. The Son (Moses 5:15)
2. The Eternal God (Doctrine & Covenants 121:32)
3. The Father, and the Son, and the Holy Ghost (3 Nephi 11:27)
4. The Father and I are One (3 Nephi 28:10)
5. He Who Hath Perfected For ever Them that are Sanctified (Hebrews 10:14)
6. He Who Liveth (Doctrine & Covenants 110:4)
7. The Eternal Judge (Moroni 10:34)
8. The Eternal Father of Heaven and Earth (Mosiah 15:4)
9. The Supreme Being (Doctrine & Covenants 104:7)
10. The God of Heaven (Moses 7:28)
11. The God of this People of Israel (Acts 13:17)
12. The Head of the Corner (1 Peter 2:7)
13. The Eternal Father (Doctrine & Covenants 20:77)
14. The Very Christ (2 Nephi 26:12)
15. Him Who Has Granted Salvation unto His People (Mosiah 15:18)
16. The Lord, the Redeemer of all Men (Alma 28:8)
17. The Lion of the Tribe of Judah (Revelation 5:5)
18. Majesty on High (Hebrews 1:3)
19. Majesty (Hebrews 8:1)
20. The Master of the Vineyard (Jacob 5:7)
21. Omegus, even Jesus Christ your Lord (Doctrine & Covenants 95:17)
22. The Mediator Between God and Men (1 Timothy 2:5)
23. Alphus (Doctrine & Covenants 95:17)
24. The Life of Men and the Light of Men (Doctrine & Covenants 93:9)
25. The Rock of their Salvation (Jacob 7:25)
26. The Light which Shineth in Darkness (Doctrine & Covenants 6:21)
27. King of Glory (Psalms 24:7)
28. Him Who Appears in the Presence of God for Us (Hebrews 9:24)
29. Him Which Delivereth us From the Wrath to Come (1 Thessalonians 1:10)

March

1. The Everlasting Father (Isaiah 9:6)
2. God Manifest in the Flesh (1 Timothy 3:16)
3. Him Who Ever Liveth to Make Intercession (Hebrews 7:25)
4. He is True, and Teaches the Way of God in Truth (Matthew 22:6)
5. He that Cometh in the Name of the Lord (Matthew 21:9)
6. He That is Holy (Revelation 3:7)
7. The Holy One (Isaiah 43:15)
8. Holy, Harmless and Undefiled, Separate from Sinners, and Made Higher than the Heavens (Hebrews 7:26)
9. The Hope of Glory (Colossians 1:27)
10. Immanuel (Doctrine & Covenants 128:22)
11. Jesus Our Lord (Romans 4:24)
12. The Judge of All (Hebrews 12:23)
13. A Priest Forever after the Order of Melchizedek (Psalms 110:4)
14. He who was Tempted in all Points as we Are (Hebrews 4:15)
15. The Wisdom, Righteousness, Sanctification, and Redemption unto Us (1 Corinthians 1:30)
16. My Light and my Salvation (Psalms 27:1)
17. JAH (Psalms 68:3)
18. One God and One Shepherd over All (1 Nephi 13:41)
19. Shepherd (Psalms 23:1)
20. He That Liveth For Ever and Ever (Revelation 4:9)
21. The Beginning of the Creation of God (Revelation 3:14)
22. The Rock of our Redeemer, Who is Christ, the Son of God (Helaman 5:12)
23. He Who Suffered for Us (1 Peter 2:21)
24. Meek and Lowly (Matthew 21:5)
25. The Savior of Israel (Acts 13:23)
26. Our Peace (Ephesians 2:14)
27. The Same Yesterday, Today, and Forever (Hebrews 13:8)
28. The Begotten of the Father (John 1:14)
29. The Beloved Son (2 Nephi 31:11)
30. Man of Counsel is My Name (Moses 7:35)
31. The Word of the Lord (Joshua 22:9)

April

1 The Same Light that Quickeneth your Understanding (Doctrine & Covenants 88:11)
2 The Fear of Isaac (Genesis 31:42)
3 He Who was Prepared from the Foundation of the World to Redeem My People (Ether 3:14)
4 The Holy Messiah (2 Nephi 2:6)
5 The Light and the Life of the World (Doctrine & Covenants 34:2)
6 King of Zion (Moses 7:53)
7 In all Things (Doctrine & Covenants 88:41)
8 Endless and Eternal is My Name (Moses 7:35)
9 Chosen of God and Precious (1 Peter 2:4)
10 God and the Father of our Lord Jesus Christ (Colossians 1:3)
11 Blood of Jesus Christ Cleanseth us from all Sin (1 John 1:7)
12 By Whom God Made the Worlds (Hebrews 1:2)
13 God the Father and the Lord Jesus Christ our Saviour (Titus 1:4)
14 Hath an Unchangeable Priesthood (Hebrews 7:24)
15 Hath Given us Understanding that we may Know Him that is True (1 John 5:20)
16 Eternal Redemption for Us (Hebrews 9:12)
17 He is Above all Things, and is Through all Things, and is Round about all Things (Doctrine & Covenants 88:41)
18 El-elohe-Israel (Genesis 33:20)
19 He is in the Sun, and the Light of the Sun, and the Power thereof by which it was Made (Doctrine & Covenants 88:7)
20 The Lord is among Us (Joshua 22:31)
21 The Just Lord (Zephaniah 3:5)
22 He Who Came unto His Own (Doctrine & Covenants 88:48)
23 Him that is True (1 John 5:20)
24 I am the Lord thy God (2 Nephi 8:16)
25 I am the True Light that is in You (Doctrine & Covenants 88:50)
26 I am the Father and the Son (Ether 3:14)
27 God our Father and Jesus Christ our Lord (2 Timothy 1:2)
28 He that Giveth Salvation unto Kings (Psalms 144:10)
29 In Whom is Salvation (2 Timothy 2:10)
30 Left us an Example (1 Peter 2:21)

May

1 The Light of Christ (Doctrine & Covenants 88:7)
2 The Light which Shineth, which Giveth you Light (Doctrine & Covenants 88:11)
3 Lord God of Abraham, Isaac, and of Israel (1 Chronicles 29:18)
4 Lord God of Israel our Father (1 Chronicles 29:10)
5 The Name of the Lord (Genesis 4:26)
6 His Arrow Shall go Forth as the Lightning (Zechariah 9:14)
7 Made of a Woman (Galatians 4:4)
8 Made under the Law (Galatians 4:4)
9 My Strength, and my Fortress, and my Refuge in the Day of Affliction (Jeremiah 16:19)
10 Of Whom are all Things (1 Corinthians 8:6)
11 One Body (1 Corinthians 12:12)
12 Our Life (Colossians 3:4)
13 Potter (Isaiah 64:8)
14 The Prophet (John 7:40)
15 A Rock of Offense (1 Peter 2:8)
16 Our Savior (1 Timothy 2:3)
17 Separate from Sinners (Hebrews 7:26)
18 Thou, Whose Name alone is Jehovah, at the Most High over all the Earth (Psalms 83:18)
19 He Shall Appear the Second Time without Sin unto Salation (Hebrews 9:23)
20 A Stone of Stumbling (1 Peter 2:8)
21 The Light which is in all Things, which Giveth Life to all Things (Doctrine & Covenants 88:13)
22 Elohim (Bible Dictionary, p. 661)
23 Thy Name is from Everlasting (Isaiah 63:16)
24 The True Light (1 John 2:8)
25 The True Vine (John 15:1)
26 The Voice of One Crying in the Wilderness (Doctrine & Covenants 88:66)
27 He Who Shall Judge the Quick and the Dead (2 Timothy 4:1)
28 He Who Knew no Sin (2 Corinthians 5:21)
29 He Who is Passed into the Heavens (Hebrews 4:14)
30 Your Father, and your God, and my God (Doctrine & Covenants 88:75)
31 A Voice of Thunderings (Doctrine & Covenants 88:90)

June

1. The Voice of Lightnings (Doctrine & Covenants 88:90)
2. The Voice of Tempests (Doctrine & Covenants 88:90)
3. The Voice of the Waves of the Sea Heaving Themselves Beyond their Bounds. (Doctrine & Covenants 88:90)
4. My Son (Psalms 2:7)
5. Through all Things (Doctrine & Covenants 88:41)
6. Round about all Things (Doctrine & Covenants 88:41)
7. Confidence of all the Ends of the Earth (Psalms 65:5)
8. A Shepherd in the Land (Zechariah 11:16)
9. Horn of David (Psalms 132:17)
10. Another Comforter (John 14:6)
11. A Light that is Endless (Mosiah 16:9)
12. El (Bible Dictionary, p. 661)
13. King of Israel (Matthew 27:42)
14. Lord of Sabaoth (Doctrine & Covenants 95:7)
15. Lord Omnipotent (Mosiah 3:5)
16. Lord's Christ (Luke 2:26)
17. Light and my Salvation (Psalms 27:1)
18. Son of Abraham (Matthew 1:1)
19. Lord God of Israel (Luke 1:68)
20. Able to Deliver Us (1 Nephi 4:3)
21. Above All (1 Nephi 11:6)
22. Blessed God (Alma 19:29)
23. Blessed Jesus (Alma 19:29)
24. Born of a Woman (Alma 19:13)
25. Branch of the Lord (2 Nephi 14:2)
26. King Immanuel (Doctrine & Covenants 128:22)
27. Christ - For so Shall He be Called (Mosiah 15:21)
28. Christ, the Lord God Omnipotent (Mosiah 5:15)
29. Christ the Lord (Mosiah 16:15)
30. Christ the Son (Alma 11:44)

July

1. Christ, Who has Broken the Bands of Death (Mosiah 15:23)
2. The Condescension of God (1 Nephi 11:26)
3. The Father of all Things (Mosiah 7:27)
4. A Fire (2 Nephi 20:17)
5. A Flame (2 Nephi 20:17)
6. He is Full of Grace and Truth (2 Nephi 2:6)
7. The God and Rock of their Salvation (Jacob 7:25)
8. God is Mindful of every People (Alma 26:37)
9. God is with Us (Alma 56:46)
10. The God of Israel, Who is the Lord of Hosts (1 Nephi 20:2)
11. A God of Miracles (2 Nephi 28:6)
12. The God of Nature (1 Nephi 18:12)
13. The God of our Fathers (1 Nephi 19:10)
14. God will Deliver Us (Alma 58:37)
15. Great Mediator of all Men (2 Nephi 2:27)
16. A Great Spirit (Alma 18:26)
17. The Great Spirit (Alma 18:3)
18. This Great Spirit, Who is God (Alma 18:28)
19. That Great Spirit, Who knows all Things (Alma 18:18)
20. He Shall be Called by the Name of Christ (Mosiah 5:9)
21. He Shall be Called the Son of God (Mosiah 15:2)
22. He that Hath Cut Rahab (2 Nephi 8:9)
23. Him that Bringeth Good Tidings (Mosiah 15:18)
24. His Word (2 Nephi 19:8)
25. Holy God (2 Nephi 9:39)
26. Holy, Holy God (Alma 31:15)
27. I am a God of Miracles (2 Nephi 27:23)
28. I am He that Comforteth You (2 Nephi 8:12)
29. I the Lord thy God am a Jealous God (Mosiah 13:13)
30. I was in the Beginning with the Father, and am the Firstborn (Doctrine & Covenants 93:21)
31. I am He; I am the First, and I am also the Last (1 Nephi 20:12)

August

1. Jesus Christ, the Son of God (2 Nephi 25:19)
2. I am Jesus Christ, the Son of God, Who was Crucified for the Sins of the World (Doctrine & Covenants 35:2)
3. I, the Lord (1 Nephi 20:15)
4. In the Beginning the Word was, for He was the Word, even the Messenger of Salvation (Doctrine & Covenants 93:8)
5. The Only Begotten of the Father, Full of Grace and Truth, even the Spirit of Truth (Doctrine & Covenants 93:11)
6. I am Jesus Christ, Who Cometh Quickly, in an Hour you Think Not (Doctrine & Covenants 51:20)
7. I am the Lord your God Dwelling in Zion, My Holy Mountain (Joel 3:17)
8. Jesus Christ, Who shall Come (Alma 45:4)
9. I, Jesus Christ, your Lord and your God, and your Redeemer (Doctrine & Covenants 18:47)
10. Jesus, thou Son of God (Alma 36:18)
11. A Just God (Alma 29:4)
12. A Life which is Endless (Mosiah 16:9)
13. Your Light in the Wilderness (1 Nephi 17:13)
14. My Fortress and my Deliverer (2 Samuel 2:22)
15. Advocate (1 John 2:1)
16. The Truth of God (2 Nephi 28:28)
17. My Deliverer and my Shield (Psalms 144:2)
18. The Lord God, the God of Abraham, the God of Isaac, and the God of Jacob (Alma 29:11)
19. The Lord is Near (2 Nephi 7:8)
20. The Lord is with Thee (1 Nephi 17:55)
21. The Lord of Hosts is My Name (2 Nephi 8:15)
22. The Most High God, Possessor of Heaven and Earth (Genesis 14:19)
23. The Lord our God, Who has Redeemed us and Made us Free (Alma 58:41)
24. The Lord your God, even Alpha and Omega, the Beginning and the End, Whose Course is One Eternal Round, the Same Today as Yesterday, and Forever, your God and your Redeemer (Doctrine & Covenants 35:1)
25. The Lord your God, even Jesus Christ, the Great I Am, Alpha and Omega, the Beginning and the End, the Same which Looked upon the Wide Expanse of Eternity, and all the Seraphic Hosts of Heaven, Before the World was Made (Doctrine & Covenants 38:1)
26. Merciful is our God (Alma 24:15)
27. I, the Lord, am Merciful and Gracious unto Those who Fear Me, and Delight to Honor those who Serve Me in Righteousness and in Truth unto the End (Doctrine & Covenants 76:5)
28. Mightier than all the Earth (1 Nephi 4:1)

29 He is Mightier than I (1 Nephi 10:8)
30 My God (2 Nephi 4:20)
31 One Eternal Round, the Same Today as Yesterday and Forever, your God (Doctrine & Covenants 35:1)

September

1. My Great God (Alma 24:8)
2. My Name's Sake (1 Nephi 20:9)
3. My Strength (1 Nephi 21:5)
4. The Name of Christ, or of God (Mosiah 25:23)
5. One Among you Whom ye Know Not (1 Nephi 10:8)
6. There is but One God (Alma 11:35)
7. They are One God (Mosiah 15:4)
8. One Messiah (2 Nephi 25:18)
9. The Only Begotten of the Father, Full of Grace, Equity, and Truth, Full of Patience Mercy, and Long-suffering (Alma 9:26)
10. Our Great God (Alma 24:7)
11. The Peace of God (Alma 7:27)
12. The Redeemer of all Men (Alma 28:8)
13. My Rock and mine Everlasting God (2 Nephi 4:35)
14. The Rock from whence ye are Hewn (2 Nephi 8:1)
15. The Rock of my Righteousness (2 Nephi 4:35)
16. The Salvation of the Lord (1 Nephi 19:17)
17. Salvation unto the Ends of the Earth (1 Nephi 21:6)
18. I am the Same that Spake unto you from the Beginning (Doctrine & Covenants 8:12)
19. I am the Same which have taken the Zion of Enoch into Mine own Bosom (Doctrine & Covenants 38:4)
20. I am the same which Spake, and the world was Made, and all Things Came by Me (Doctrine & Covenants 38:3)
21. The Son of our Great God (Alma 24:13)
22. The Son of the Everlasting God (1 Nephi 11:32)
23. The Son, the Only Begotten of the Father (Alma 5:48)
24. Thou art my God (Hosea 2:23)
25. Standard (1 Nephi 21:22)
26. The Stone upon which they might Build and have Safe Foundation (Jacob 4:15)
27. My Support (2 Nephi 4:20)
28. That God Who Brought the Children of Israel out of the Land of Egypt (Mosiah 7:19)
29. That God Who was the God of Abraham, and Isaac, and Jacob (Mosiah 7:19)
30. There is None other Name given under Heaven Save it be this Jesus Christ (2 Nephi 25:20)

October

1. Thou art Angry, O Lord (Alma 33:16)
2. Thou art God (Alma 22:18)
3. Thou art Merciful, O God (Alma 33:4)
4. True and Faithful (2 Nephi 31:15)
5. The True and Living God (1 Nephi 17:30)
6. The Lord and His Goodness (Hosea 3:5)
7. The Very God of Israel (1 Nephi 19:7)
8. Our Great and Eternal Head (Helaman 13:38)
9. The Voice of the Lord (3 Nephi 1:12)
10. The Power and Spirit of God, which was in Jesus Christ (3 Nephi 7:21)
11. I am in the Father, and the Father in Me (3 Nephi 9:15)
12. With the Father from the Beginning (3 Nephi 9:15)
13. The Lord God of Israel was their Inheritance (Joshua 13:33)
14. I, and the Holy Ghost are One (3 Nephi 11:36)
15. One (Doctrine & Covenants 50:43)
16. I am He that Gave the Law (3 Nephi 15:5)
17. I am He who Covenanted with my People Israel (3 Nephi 15:5)
18. My Rock (3 Nephi 18:12)
19. I am the Light which ye shall Hold Up (3 Nephi 18:24)
20. I am He of whom Moses Spake (3 Nephi 20:23)
21. The God of Israel Shall be your Rearward (3 Nephi 20:42)
22. Thy Maker, thy Husband, the Lord of Hosts is His Name (3 Nephi 22:5)
23. The Lord that hath Mercy on Thee (3 Nephi 22:10)
24. I will be a Swift Witness (3 Nephi 24:5)
25. The Son of Righteousness (3 Nephi 25:2)
26. Christ, Who was before the World Began (3 Nephi 26:5)
27. Christ for their Shepherd (Mormon 5:17)
28. The Very Christ and the Very God (Mormon 3:21)
29. The Eternal Father of Heaven (Mormon 6:22)
30. Jesus Christ, even the Father and the Son (Mormon 9:12)
31. The Holiness of Jesus Christ (Mormon 9:5)

November

1. An Unchangeable Being (Mormon 9:31)
2. Almighty Power (Mormon 9:26)
3. God of our Salvation (Psalms 65:5)
4. The Father of the Heavens and of the Earth, and all Things that in Them Are (Ether 4:7)
5. I am He Who Speaketh (Ether 4:8)
6. I am the Father (Ether 4:12)
7. I am the Same that Leadeth Men to all Good (Ether 4:12)
8. The Truth of the World (Ether 4:9)
9. It is I that hath Spoken it (Ether 4:19)
10. The Gift of His Son (Ether 12:11)
11. A More Excellent Way (Ether 12:11)
12. The Finisher of their Faith (Moroni 6:4)
13. Son Ahman; or, in other words, Alphus (D&C 95:17)
14. Jesus is the Christ (Moroni 7:44)
15. His Son, Jesus Christ (Moroni 7:48)
16. He is Pure (Moroni 7:48)
17. His Holy Child, Jesus (Moroni 8:3)
18. He is Unchangeable from all Eternity to all Eternity (Moroni 8:18)
19. Our Lord Jesus Christ, Who Sitteth on the Right Hand of His Power (Moroni 9:26)
20. A Voice (3 Nephi 9:1)
21. The Founder of Peace (Mosiah 15:18)
22. The Only Wise and True God, and Jesus Christ, Whom He hath Sent (Doctrine & Covenants 132:24)
23. Received the Fulness of the Father (Doctrine & Covenants 76:71)
24. The Same Unchangeable God (Doctrine & Covenants 20:17)
25. Redemption (1 Corinthians 1:30)
26. I am the True Light that Lighteth every Man that Cometh into the World (Doctrine & Covenants 93:2)
27. I am With the Faithful Always (Doctrine & Covenants 62:9)
28. Your Father which is in Heaven (Doctrine & Covenants 84:92)
29. I am He Who said Other Sheep have I Which are not of this Fold (Doctrine & Covenants 10:59)
30. From Everlasting to Everlasting (Doctrine & Covenants 20:17)

December

1. God is Merciful (Doctrine & Covenants 2:10)
2. I am He Who Spake in Righteousness (Doctrine & Covenants 133:47)
3. Him Who has Ordained you from on High (Doctrine & Covenants 77:2)
4. I am He Who was Slain (Doctrine & Covenants 110:4)
5. I, the Lord, am Merciful (Doctrine & Covenants 70:18)
6. I am the Life and the Light of the World (Doctrine & Covenants 11:28)
7. A Light which Cannot be Hid in Darkness (Doctrine & Covenants 14:9)
8. Like Fuller's Soap (Doctrine & Covenants 128:24)
9. The Lord God, the Mighty One of Israel (Doctrine & Covenants 36:1)
10. The Lord is God, and Beside Him there is no Savior (Doctrine & Covenants 76:1)
11. The Lord your God, even Jesus Christ, your Advocate, Who Knoweth the Weakness of Man and how to Succor them who are Tempted (Doctrine & Covenants 62:1)
12. He is a Man like Ourselves (Doctrine & Covenants 129:1)
13. A Refiner and Purifier of Silver (Doctrine & Covenants 128:24)
14. The Voice of the Day of the Lord (Zephaniah 1:14)
15. The Same which Came in the Meridian of Time unto Mine Own, and Mine Own Received me Not (Doctrine & Covenants 39:3)
16. The Same which Knoweth all Things, for all Things are Present before Mine Eyes (Doctrine & Covenants 38:2)
17. He was the Word, even the Messenger of Salvation (Doctrine & Covenants 93:8)
18. Your Father, Who is in Heaven (Doctrine & Covenants 84:83)
19. Alpha and Omega, your Lord and your God (Doctrine & Covenants 75:1)
20. The Framer of Heaven and Earth, and all Things which are in Them (Doctrine & Covenants 20:17)
21. Him Who Sitteth upon the Throne, even the Lamb (Doctrine & Covenants 88:115)
22. Alpha and Omega, even Jesus Christ (Doctrine & Covenants 81:7)
23. A Light which Shineth in Darkness and the Darkness Comprehendeth it Not (Doctrine & Covenants 39:2)
24. The Marvelous Light of God (Mosiah 27:29)
25. A Light to the Gentiles (1 Nephi 21:6)
26. Perfect (3 Nephi 12:48)
27. A Child (2 Nephi 19:6)
28. Eternal King (Doctrine & Covenants 128:23)
29. A Sacrifice for Sin (2 Nephi 2:7)
30. That Great High Priest, That is Passed into the Heavens (Hebrews 4:14)
31. He is the Same, and His Years never Fail (Doctrine & Covenants 76:4)

Minute Musings

Spontaneous Combustions of Thought

Volume Two

Appendix Two

An Alphabetical List of
366 Scriptural References to Jesus Christ

"That which cometh from above is sacred, and must be
spoken with care, and by constraint of the Spirit."
(Doctrine & Covenants 63:64).

compiled by

Philip M. Hudson

A
Able to Deliver Us (1 Nephi 4:3) (June 20)
Above All (1 Nephi 11:6) (June 21)
Almighty Power (Mormon 9:26) (November 2)
Alpha and Omega, even Jesus Christ (Doctrine & Covenants 81:7) (December 22)
Alpha and Omega, your Lord and your God (Doctrine & Covenants 75:1) (December 19)
Alphus (Doctrine & Covenants 95:17) (February 23)
Advocate (1 John 2:1) (August 15)
Angry, O Lord (Alma 33:16) (October 1)
Another Comforter (John 14:6) (June 10)
Appears in the Presence of God (Hebrews 9:24) (February 28)
Arrow Shall go forth as the Lightning (Zechariah 9:14) (May 6)

B
Beginning of the Creation of God (Revelation 3:14) (March 21)
Begotten of the Father (John 1:14) (March 28)
Beloved Son (2 Nephi 31:11) (March 29)
Blessed God (Alma 19:29) (June 22)
Blessed Jesus (Alma 19:29) (June 23)
Blood of Jesus Christ Cleanseth us from all Sin (1 John 1:7) (April 11)
Born of a Woman (Alma 19:13) (June 24)
Branch of the Lord (2 Nephi 14:2) (June 25)
By Whom God Made the Worlds (Hebrews 1:2) (April 12)

C
Child (2 Nephi 19:6) (December 27)
Chosen of God and Precious (1 Peter 2:4) (April 9)
Christ - for so Shall He be Called (Mosiah 15:21) (June 27)
Christ for their Shepherd (Mormon 5:17) (October 27)
Christ, the Eternal God (2 Nephi 26:12) (January 7)
Christ the Lord (Mosiah 16:15) (June 29)
Christ, the Lord God Omnipotent (Mosiah 5:15) (June 28)
Christ the Power of God and the Wisdom of God (1 Corinthians 1:24) (January 20)
Christ the Son (Alma 11:44) (June 30)
Christ, Who has Broken the Bands of Death (Mosiah 15:23) (July 1)
Christ, Who was before the World Began (3 Nephi 26:5) (October 26)
Condescension of God (1 Nephi 11:26) (July 2)
Confidence of all the Ends of the Earth (Psalms 65:5) (June 7)

D
Delivereth us From the Wrath to Come (1 Thessalonians 1:10) (February 29)

E

El (Bible Dictionary, p. 661) (June 12)
El-elohe-Israel (Genesis 33:20) (April 18)
Elohim (Bible Dictionary, p. 661) (May 22)
Endless and Eternal is My Name (Moses 7:35) (April 8)
Eternal Father (Doctrine & Covenants 20:77) (February 13)
Eternal Father of Heaven (Mormon 6:22) (October 29)
Eternal Father of Heaven and Earth (Mosiah 15:4) (February 8)
Eternal God (Doctrine & Covenants 121:32) (February 2)
Eternal Judge of Both Quick and Dead (Moroni 10:34) (February 7)
Eternal King (Doctrine & Covenants 128:23) (December 28)
Eternal Redemption for Us (Hebrews 9:12) (April 16)
Everlasting Father (Isaiah 9:6) (March 1)
Ever Liveth to Make Intercession (Hebrews 7:25) (March 3)

F

Father and I are One (3 Nephi 28:10) (February 4)
Father, and the Son, and the Holy Ghost (3 Nephi 11:27) (February 3)
Father of all Things (Mosiah 7:27) (July 3)
Father of the Heavens and of the Earth, and all Things that in them Are
    (Ether 4:7) (November 4)
Fear of Isaac (Genesis 31:42) (April 2)
Figure for the Time then Present (Hebrews 9:9) (January 14)
Finisher of their Faith (Moroni 6:4) (November 12)
Fire (2 Nephi 20:17) (July 4)
Firstborn from the Dead (Colossians 1:18) (June 11)
Flame (2 Nephi 20:17) (July 5)
Founder of Peace (Mosiah 15:18) (November 21)
Framer of Heaven and Earth, and All Things which are in Them
    (Doctrine & Covenants 20:17) (December 20)
From Everlasting to Everlasting (Doctrine & Covenants 20:17) (November 30)
Full of Grace and Truth (2 Nephi 2:6) (July 6)

G

Gift of His Son (Ether 12:11) (November 10)
God and Rock of their Salvation (Jacob 7:25) (July 7)
God and the Father of our Lord Jesus Christ (Colossians 1:3) (April 10)
God in the Highest (Luke 2:14) (January 29)
God is Merciful (Doctrine & Covenants 2:10) (December 1)
God is Mindful of every People (Alma 26:37) (July 8)
God is with Us (Alma 56:46) (July 9)
God Manifest in the Flesh (1 Timothy 3:16) (March 2)
God of Glory (Moses 1:20) (January 9)

God of Gods (Deuteronomy 10:17) (January 28)
God of Heaven (Moses 7:28) (February 10)
God of Israel Shall be your Rearward (3 Nephi 20:42) (October 21)
God of Israel, Who is the Lord of Hosts (1 Nephi 20:2) (July 10)
God of Miracles (2 Nephi 28:6) (July 11)
God of Nature (1 Nephi 18:12) (July 12)
God of our Fathers (1 Nephi 19:10) (July 13)
God of our Salvation (Psalms 65:5) (November 3)
God of this People of Israel (Acts 13:17) (February 11)
God our Father and Jesus Christ our Lord (2 Timothy 1:2) (April 27)
God the Eternal Father (Doctrine & Covenants 20:77) (January 5)
God the Father and the Lord Jesus Christ our Saviour (Titus 1:4) (April 13)
God Who Brought the Children of Israel out of the Land of Egypt.
    (Mosiah 7:19) (September 28)
God Who was the God of Abraham, and Isaac, and Jacob (Mosiah 7:19) (September 29)
God will Deliver Us (Alma 58:37) (July 14)
Granted Salvation unto His People (Mosiah 15:18) (February 15)
Great and Eternal Head (Helaman 13:38) (October 8)
Great High Priest, That is Passed into the Heavens (Hebrews 4:14) (December 30)
Great Mediator (2 Nephi 2:28) (July 15)
Great Mediator of all Men (2 Nephi 2:27) (January 13)
[A] Great Spirit (Alma 18:26) (July 16)
[The] Great Spirit (Alma 18:3) (July 17)
[This] Great Spirit, Who is God (Alma 18:28) (July 18)
[That] Great Spirit, Who Knows all Things (Alma 18:18) (July 19)

H
Hath an Unchangeable Priesthood (Hebrews 7:24) (April 14)
Hath Given us Understanding that we may Know Him that is True (1 John 5:20)
    (April 15)
He is a Man like Ourselves (Doctrine & Covenants 129:1) (December 12)
He is Above all Things, and In all Things, and is Through all Things, and is Round about all Things (Doctrine & Covenants 88:41) (April 17)
He is in the Moon, and is the Light of the Moon, and the Power Thereof by which it was Made (Doctrine & Covenants 88:8) (April 18)
He is in the Sun, and the Light of the Sun, and the Power thereof by which it was
    Made (Doctrine & Covenants 88:7) (April 19)
He is Pure (Moroni 7:48) (November 16)
He is the Same, and His Years never Fail (Doctrine & Covenants 76:4) (December 31)
He Shall be Called by the Name of Christ (Mosiah 5:9) (July 20)
He Shall be Called the Son of God (Mosiah 15:2) (July 21)
He That Cometh in the Name of the Lord (Matthew 21:9) (March 5)
He that Giveth Salvation unto Kings (Psalms 144:10) (April 28)

He that Hath the Key of David (Revelation 3:7) (April 21)
He that Hath Cut Rahab (2 Nephi 8:9) (July 22)
He That is Holy (Revelation 3:7) (March 6)
He Who Came unto his Own (Doctrine & Covenants 88:48) (April 22)
Head of the Corner (1 Peter 2:7) (February 12)
Him that Bringeth Good Tidings (Mosiah 15:18) (July 23)
Him that hath Called us to Glory and Virtue (2 Peter 1:3) (January 27)
Him that is True (1 John 5:20) (April 23)
Him Who has Ordained you from on High (Doctrine & Covenants 77:2) (December 3)
His Holy Child, Jesus (Moroni 8:3) (November 17)
His Holy Will (Moroni 7:2) (November 13)
His Son, Jesus Christ (Moroni 7:48) (November 15)
His Word (2 Nephi 19:8) (July 24)
Holiness of Jesus Christ (Mormon 9:5) (October 31)
Holy God (2 Nephi 9:39) (July 25)
Holy, Harmless [and] Undefiled, Separate from Sinners,
    and Made Higher Than the Heavens (Hebrews 7:26) (March 8)
Holy, Holy God (Alma 31:15) (July 26)
Holy Messiah (2 Nephi 2:6) (April 4)
Holy One (Isaiah 43:15) (March 7)
Hope of Glory (Colossians 1:27) (March 9)
Horn of David (Psalms 132:17) (June 9)

I
I am a God of Miracles (2 Nephi 27:23) (July 27)
I am God (Moses 7:35) (January 19)
I am He; I am the First, and I am also the Last (1 Nephi 20:12) (July 31)
I am He of whom Moses Spake (3 Nephi 20:23) (October 20)
I am He that Comforteth You (2 Nephi 8:12) (July 28)
I am in the Father, and the Father in Me (3 Nephi 9:15) (October 11)
I am He that Gave the Law (3 Nephi 15:5) (October 16)
I am He who Covenanted with my People Israel (3 Nephi 15:5) (October 17)
I am He Who said Other Sheep have I Which are not of this Fold
    (Doctrine & Covenants 10:59) (November 29)
I am He Who spake in Righteousness (Doctrine & Covenants 133:47) (December 2)
I am He Who Speaketh (Ether 4:8) (November 5)
I am He Who was Slain (Doctrine & Covenants 110:4) (December 4)
I am in the Father, and the Father in Me (3 Nephi 9:15) (October 11)
I am Jesus Christ, the Son of God, Who was Crucified for the Sins of the World
    (Doctrine & Covenants 35:2) (August 2)
I am Jesus Christ, the Son of the Living God, Who Created the Heavens and the Earth
    (Doctrine & Covenants 14:9) (August 5)

I am Jesus Christ, Who Cometh Quickly, in an Hour you Think Not
    (Doctrine & Covenants 51:20) (August 6)
I am the Father (Ether 4:12) (November 6)
I am the Father and the Son (Ether 3:14) (April 26)
I am the God of Israel, and the God of the Whole Earth (3 Nephi 11:14) (October 13)
I am the Life and the Light of the World (Doctrine & Covenants 11:28) (December 6)
I am the Light which ye shall Hold Up (3 Nephi 18:24) (October 19)
I am the Lord thy God (2 Nephi 8:16) (April 24)
I am the Lord your God dwelling in Zion, My Holy Mountain (Joel 3:17) (August 7)
I am the Same that Leadeth Men to all Good (Ether 4:12) (November 7)
I am the True Light that is in You (Doctrine & Covenants 88:50) (April 25)
I am the True Light that Lighteth every Man that Cometh into the World
    (Doctrine & Covenants 93:2) (November 26)
I am with the Faithful Always (Doctrine & Covenants 62:9) (November 27)
I, and the Holy Ghost are One (3 Nephi 11:36) (October 14)
I, God (Doctrine & Covenants 19:16) (January 18)
I, Jesus Christ, your Lord and your God, and your Redeemer
    (Doctrine & Covenants 18:47) (August 9)
I, the Lord (1 Nephi 20:15) (August 3)
I, the Lord, am Merciful (Doctrine & Covenants 70:18) (December 5)
I, the Lord, am Merciful and Gracious unto Those who Fear Me, and Delight to
    Honor those who Serve me in Righteousness and in Truth unto the End
    (Doctrine & Covenants 76:5) (August 27)
I, the Lord God (Moses 3:6) (January 23)
I the Lord thy God am a Jealous God (Mosiah 13:13) (July 29)
I was in the Beginning with the Father, and am the Firstborn
    (Doctrine & Covenants 93:21) (July 30)
I will be their God (Ezekiel 11:20) (November 14)
Immanuel (Doctrine & Covenants 128:22) (March 10)
In all Things (Doctrine & Covenants 88:41) (April 7)
In the Beginning the Word was, for He was the Word, even the Messenger of
    Salvation (Doctrine & Covenants 93:8) (August 4)
In whom is Salvation (2 Timothy 2:10) (April 29)
It is I that hath Spoken it (Ether 4:19) (November 9)

J
JAH (Psalms 68:3) (March 17)
Jesus Christ, even the Father and the Son (Mormon 9:12) (October 30)
Jesus Christ, the Son of God (2 Nephi 25:19) (August 1)
Jesus Christ the Son of the Living God, the Savior of the World
    (Doctrine & Covenants 42:1) (August 4)
Jesus is the Christ (Moroni 7:44) (November 14)
Jesus is the Very Christ (2 Nephi 26:12) (January 22)

Jesus our Lord (Romans 4:24) (March 11)
Jesus, the Mediator of the New Covenant (Doctrine & Covenants 107:19) (January 3)
Jesus, thou Son of God (Alma 36:18) (August 10)
Judge of All (Hebrews 12:23) (March 12)
Just God (Alma 29:4) (August 11)
Just Lord (Zephaniah 3:5) (April 21)

K
King Immanuel (Doctrine & Covenants 128:22) (June 26)
King of Glory (Psalms 24:7) (February 27)
King of Israel (Matthew 27:42) (June 13)
King of Zion (Moses 7:53) (April 6)

L
Left us an Example (1 Peter 2:21) (April 30)
Life of Men and the Light of Men (Doctrine & Covenants 93:9) (February 24)
Life which is Endless (Mosiah 16:9) (August 12)
Light and my Salvation (Psalms 27:1) (June 17)
Light and the Life of the World (Doctrine & Covenants 34:2) (April 5)
Light in the Wilderness (1 Nephi 17:13) (August 13)
Light of Christ (Doctrine & Covenants 88:7) (May 1)
Light of the Sun, and the Power Thereof by Which it Was Made
    (Doctrine & Covenants 88:7) (June 8)
Light to the Gentiles (1 Nephi 21:6) (December 25)
Light that is Endless (Mosiah 16:9) (June 11)
Light which Cannot be Hid in Darkness (Doctrine & Covenants 14:9) (December 7)
Light which is in all Things, which Giveth Life to all Things
    (Doctrine & Covenants 88:13) (May 21)
Light which Shineth in Darkness (Doctrine & Covenants 6:21) (February 26)
Light which Shineth in Darkness and the Darkness Comprehendeth it Not
    (Doctrine & Covenants 39:2) (December 23)
Light which Shineth, which Giveth you Light (Doctrine & Covenants 88:11) (May 2)
Like Fuller's Soap (Doctrine & Covenants 128:24) (December 8)
Lion of the Tribe of Judah (Revelation 5:5) (February 17)
Liveth (Doctrine & Covenants 110:4) (February 6)
Liveth For Ever and Ever (Revelation 4:9) (March 20)
Lord, Even the Savior (Doctrine & Covenants 133:25) (January 1)
Lord God of Abraham, Isaac, and of Israel (1 Chronicles 29:18) (May 3)
Lord God of Israel (Luke 1:68) (June 19)
Lord God of Israel our Father (1 Chronicles 29:10) (May 4)
Lord God of Israel was their Inheritance (Joshua 13:33) (October 13)
Lord God, the God of Abraham, the God of Isaac, and the God of Jacob
    (Alma 29:11) (August 18)

Lord God, the Mighty One of Israel (Doctrine & Covenants 36:1) (December 9)
Lord and His Goodness (Hosea 3:5) (October 6)
Lord is among Us (Joshua 22:31) (April 20)
Lord is God, and Beside Him there is no Savior (Doctrine & Covenants 76:1) (December 10)
Lord is Near (2 Nephi 7:8) (August 19)
Lord is with Thee (1 Nephi 17:55) (August 20)
Lord Jesus Christ the Son of the Father (2 Nephi 11:32) (January 4)
Lord of Hosts is My Name (2 Nephi 8:15) (August 21)
Lord of Sabaoth (Doctrine & Covenants 95:7) (June 14)
Lord Omnipotent (Mosiah 3:5) (June 15)
Lord our God (Alma 15:10) (August 22)
Lord our God, Who has Redeemed us and Made us Free (Alma 58:41) (August 23)
Lord that hath Mercy on Thee (3 Nephi 22:10) (October 23)
Lord, the Redeemer of All Men (Alma 28:8) (February 16)
Lord thy God (Abraham 2:7) (January 26)
Lord will roar from Zion, and utter His Voice from Jerusalem (Amos 1:2) (August 8)
Lord your God, even Alpha and Omega, the Beginning and the End, Whose Course is one Eternal Round; the Same Today as Yesterday, and Forever, your God and your Redeemer (Doctrine & Covenants 35:1) (August 24)
The Lord your God, even Jesus Christ, the Great I Am, Alpha and Omega, the Beginning and the End, the Same which Looked upon the Wide Expanse of Eternity, and all the Seraphic Hosts of Heaven, Before the World was Made (Doctrine & Covenants 38:1) (August 25)
Lord your God, even Jesus Christ, your Advocate, Who Knoweth the Weakness of Man and how to Succor them who are Tempted (Doctrine & Covenants 62:1) (December 11)
Lord's Christ (Luke 2:26) (June 17)

M
Made of a Woman (Galatians 4:4) (May 7)
Made Under the Law (Galatians 4:4) (May 8)
Majesty (Hebrews 8:1) (February 19)
Majesty on High (Hebrews 1:3) (February 18)
Maker, thy Husband, the Lord of Hosts is His Name (3 Nephi 22:5) (October 22)
Man of Counsel is My Name (Moses 7:35) (March 30)
Man of Holiness (Moses 7:35) (January 8)
Marvelous Light of God (Mosiah 27:29) (December 24)
Master of the Vineyard (Jacob 5:7) (February 20)
Mediator between God and Men (1 Timothy 2:5) (February 22)
Meek and Lowly (Matthew 21:5) (March 24)
Merciful is our God (Alma 24:15) (August 26)
Merciful, O God (Alma 33:4) (October 3)

Merciful and Gracious unto Those who Fear Me, and Delight to Honor those who Serve me in Righteousness and in Truth unto the End (Doctrine & Covenants 76:5) (August 27)
Messenger of Salvation (Doctrine & Covenants 93:8) (January 6)
Messiah, the King of Zion, the Rock of Heaven (Moses 7:53) (January 17)
Mightier than all the Earth (1 Nephi 4:1) (August 28)
Mightier than I (1 Nephi 10:8) (August 29)
More Excellent Way (Ether 12:11) (November 11)
Most High God, Possessor of Heaven and Earth (Genesis 14:19) (August 22)
My Deliverer and my Shield (Psalms 144:2) (August 17)
My Fortress and my Deliverer (2 Samuel 2:22) (August 14)
My God (2 Nephi 4:20) (August 30)
My God, and your God (Moses 6:43) (January 30)
My Great God (Alma 24:8) (September 1)
My Light and my Salvation (Psalms 68:3) (March 16)
My Name's Sake (1 Nephi 20:9) (September 2)
My Rock (3 Nephi 18:12) (October 18)
My Son (Psalms 2:7) (June 4)
My Strength (1 Nephi 21:5) (September 3)
My Strength, and my Fortress, and my Refuge in the Day of Affliction (Jeremiah 16:19) (May 9)

N
Name is from Everlasting (Isaiah 63:16) (May 23)
Name of Christ, or of God (Mosiah 25:23) (September 4)
Name of the Lord (Genesis 4:26) (May 5)

O
Of Whom are all Things (1 Corinthians 8:6) (May 10)
Omegus, even Jesus Christ your Lord (Doctrine & Covenants 95:17) (February 21)
One (Doctrine & Covenants 50:43) (October 15)
One among you Whom ye Know Not (1 Nephi 10:8) (September 5)
One Body (1 Corinthians 12:12) (May 11)
One Eternal Round, the Same Today as Yesterday and Forever, your God and your Redeemer (Doctrine & Covenants 35:1) (August 31)
One God and One Shepherd over All (1 Nephi 13:41) (March 18)
[There is but] One God (Alma 11:35) (August 9)
[They are] One God (Mosiah 15:4) (September 7)
One Eternal Round, the Same Today as Yesterday and Forever, your God and your Redeemer (Doctrine & Covenants 35:1) (August 31)
One Messiah (2 Nephi 25:18) (September 8)
Only Begotten (Moses 3:18) (January 21)
Only Begotten, even Jesus Christ (Moses 7:50) (January 24)

Only Begotten of the Father, Full of Grace and Truth, even the Spirit of Truth (Doctrine & Covenants 93:11) (August 5)
Only Begotten of the Father, Full of Grace, Equity, and Truth, Full of Patience Mercy, and Long-suffering (Alma 9:26) (September 9)
Only Wise and True God, and Jesus Christ, Whom He hath Sent (Doctrine & Covenants 132:24) (November 22)
Our Great God (Alma 24:7) (September 10)
Our Life (Colossians 3:4) (May 12)
Our Lord Jesus Christ, Who Sitteth on the Right Hand of his Power (Moroni 9:26) (November 19)
Our Peace (Ephesians 2:14) (March 26)

P
Peace of God (Alma 7:27) (September 11)
Perfect (3 Nephi 12:48) (December 26)
Perfected For ever them that are Sanctified (Hebrews 10:14) (February 5)
Potter (Isaiah 64:8) (May 13)
Power and Spirit of God, which was in Jesus Christ (3 Nephi 7:21) (October 10)
Prepared from the Foundation of the World to Redeem My People (Ether 3:14) (April 3)
Priest Forever after the Order of Melchizedek (Psalms 110:4) (March 13)
Prince and a Savior (Acts 5:31) (January 31)
[A] Prophet (Deuteronomy 18:15) (January 12)
[The] Prophet (John 7:40) (May 14)

R
Received the Fulness of the Father (Doctrine & Covenants 76:71) (November 23)
Redeemer of all Men (Alma 28:8) (September 12)
Redemption (1 Corinthians 1:30) (November 25)
Refiner and Purifier of Silver (Doctrine & Covenants 128:24) (December 13)
Righteous (Moses 7:47) (January 25)
Rock and Mine Everlasting God (2 Nephi 4:35) (September 13)
Rock from whence ye are Hewn (2 Nephi 8:1) (September 14)
Rock of my Righteousness (2 Nephi 4:35) (September 15)
Rock of Offense (1 Peter 2:8) (May 15)
Rock of Offense to Both the Houses of Israel (Isaiah 8:14) (January 15)
Rock of our Redeemer, who is Christ, the Son of God (Helaman 5:12) (March 22)
Rock of their Salvation (Jacob 7:15) (February 25)
Rock that is Higher than I (Psalms 62:1) (January 10)
Round about all Things (Doctrine & Covenants 88:41) (June 6)

S

Sacrifice for Sin (2 Nephi 2:7) (December 29)
Salvation of the Lord (1 Nephi 19:17) (September 16)
Salvation unto the Ends of the Earth (1 Nephi 21:6) (September 17)
Same Light that Quickeneth your Understanding (Doctrine & Covenants 88:11) (April 1)
Same that Spake unto you from the Beginning (Doctrine & Covenants) (September 18)
Same Unchangeable God (Doctrine & Covenants 20:17) (November 24)
Same which Came in the Meridian of Time unto Mine Own, and Mine Own Received Me not (Doctrine & Covenants 39:3) (December 15)
Same which have taken the Zion of Enoch into Mine own Bosom (Doctrine & Covenants 38:4) (September 19)
Same which Knoweth all Things, for all Things are Present before Mine Eyes (Doctrine & Covenants 38:2) (December 16)
[I am the] Same which Spake, and the World was Made, and all Things came by Me (Doctrine & Covenants 38:3) (September 20)
Same Yesterday, Today, and Forever (Hebrews 13:8) (March 27)
Savior (1 Timothy 2:3) (May 16)
Savior of Israel (Acts 13:23) (March 25)
Separate from Sinners (Hebrews 7:26) (May 17)
Servant of the Lord, or of Jehovah (Zechariah 3:8) (May 18)
Shadow of Thing to Come (Colossians 2:17) (January 2)
Shall Appear the Second Time without Sin unto Salvation (Hebrews 9:23) (May 19)
Shepherd (Psalms 23:1) (March 19)
Shepherd in the Land (Zechariah 11:16) (June 8)
Sitteth upon the Throne, even the Lamb (Doctrine & Covenants 88:115) (December 21)
Son (Moses 5:15) (February 1)
Son Ahman; or, in other words, Alphus (Doctrine & Covenants 95:17) (November 13)
Son of Abraham (Matthew 1:1) (June 18)
Son of our Great God (Alma 24:13) (September 21)
Son of Righteousness (3 Nephi 25:2) (October 25)
Son of the Everlasting God (1 Nephi 11:32) (September 22)
Standard (1 Nephi 21:22) (September 25)
Stem of Jesse (Isaiah 11:1) (January 11)
Stone of Stumbling (1 Peter 2:8) (May 20)
Stone upon which they might Build and have Safe Foundation (Jacob 4:15) (September 26)
Stumbling Stone and Rock of Offense (Romans 9:33) (January 16)
Suffered for Us (1 Peter 2:21) (March 23)
Support (2 Nephi 4:20) (September 27)
Supreme Being (Doctrine & Covenants 104:7) (February 9)
Swift Witness (3 Nephi 24:5) (October 24)

T

Tempted in all Points as We are (Hebrews 4:15) (March 14)
There is but One God (Alma 11:35) (September 6)
There is None other Name given under Heaven Save it be this Jesus Christ (2 Nephi 25:20) (September 30)
They are One God (Mosiah 15:4) (September 7)
Thou art God (Alma 22:18) (October 2)
Thou art my God (Hosea 2:23) (September 24)
Thou, Whose Name alone is Jehovah, art the Most High over all the Earth (Psalms 83:18) (May 18)
Through all Things (Doctrine & Covenants 88:41) (June 5)
True and Faithful (2 Nephi 31:15) (October 4)
True and Living God (1 Nephi 17:30) (October 5)
True, and Teaches the Way of God in Truth (Matthew 22:6) (March 4)
True Light (1 John 2:8) (May 24)
True Vine (John 15:1) (May 25)
Truth of God (2 Nephi 28:28) (August 16)
Truth of the World (Ether 4:9) (November 8)

U

Unchangeable Being (Mormon 9:19) (November 1)
Unchangeable from all Eternity to all Eternity (Moroni 8:18) (November 18)

V

Very Christ (2 Nephi 26:12) (February 14)
Very Christ and the Very God (Mormon 3:21) (October 28)
Very God of Israel (1 Nephi 19:7) (October 7)
Voice (3 Nephi 9:1) (November 20)
Voice of Lightnings (Doctrine & Covenants 88:90) (June 1)
Voice of One Crying in the Wilderness (Doctrine & Covenants 88:66) (May 26)
Voice of Tempests (Doctrine & Covenants 88:90) (June 2)
Voice of the Day of the Lord (Zephaniah 1:14) (December 14)
Voice of the Lord (3 Nephi 1:12) (October 9)
Voice of the Waves of the Sea Heaving Themselves Beyond their Bounds (Doctrine & Covenants 88:90) (June 3)
Voice of Thunderings (Doctrine & Covenants 88:90) (May 31)

W

Who is Passed into the Heavens (Hebrews 4:14) (May 29)
Who Knew no Sin (2 Corinthians 5:21) (May 28)
Who Shall Judge the Quick and the Dead (2 Timothy 4:1) (May 27)

Wisdom, Righteousness, Sanctification, and Redemption (1 Corinthians 1:30) (March 15)
With the Father from the Beginning (3 Nephi 9:15) (October 12)
Word, Even the Messenger of Salvation (Doctrine & Covenants 93:8) (December 17)
Word of the Lord (Joshua 22:9) (March 31)

Y
Your Father, and your God, and my God (Doctrine & Covenants 88:75) (May 30)
Your Father which is in Heaven (Doctrine & Covenants 84:92) (November 28)
Your Father, Who is in Heaven (Doctrine & Covenants 84:83) (December 18)
Your Redeemer, your Lord, and your God (Doctrine & Covenants 10:70) (January 29)

Minute Musings

Spontaneous Combustions of Thought

Volume Two

Appendix Three

An Alphabetical List of
1,098 Scriptural References to Jesus Christ

"That which cometh from above is sacred, and must be
spoken with care, and by constraint of the Spirit."
(Doctrine & Covenants 63:64).

compiled by

Philip M. Hudson

A

Abba, Father
(Mark 14:36) Volume 1 - February 14
Able to Deliver Us
(1 Nephi 4:3) Volume 2 – June 20
Able to Save to the Uttermost
(Hebrews 7:25) Volume 1 - January 11
Able to Succor Them That are Tempted
(Hebrews 2:18) Volume 1 - March 1
Above All
(1 Nephi 11:6) Volume 2 – June 21
Above all Things
(Doctrine & Covenants 88:41) Volume 3 – August 30
Advocate
(1 John 2:1) Volume 2 – August 15
Advocate with the Father
(1 John 2:1) Volume 1 - May 1
All-powerful Creator of Earth
(Jacob 2:5) Volume 3 – November 29
All-powerful Creator of Heaven
(Jacob 2:5) Volume 3 – November 28
All-powerful God
(Alma 44:5) Volume 3 – May 7
All Things came by Me
(Doctrine & Covenants 38:3) Volume 3 – November 12
All-wise Creator
(Mosiah 29:19) Volume 3 – March 17
Almighty
(Revelation 1:8) Volume 1 - August 9
Almighty God
(Genesis 17:1) Volume 1 - August 21
Almighty Power
(Mormon 9:26) Volume 2 – November 2
Alpha and Omega
(Revelation 1:11) Volume 1 - July 28
Alpha and Omega, even Jesus Christ
(Doctrine & Covenants 81:7) Volume 2 – December 22
Alpha and Omega, the Beginning and the End
(Doctrine & Covenants 61:1) Volume 3 – July 28
Alpha and Omega, your Lord and your God
(Doctrine & Covenants 75:1) Volume 2 – December 19
Alphus
(Doctrine & Covenants 95:17) Volume 2 – February 23

Amen
   (John 14:6) Volume 1 - January 27
Angel of the Lord
   (Zecharaiah 3:10) Volume 3 – May 19
Angry, O Lord
   (Alma 33:16) Volume 2 – October 1
Anointed One
   (Psalms 2:2) Volume 1 - April 15
Another Comforter
   (John 14:6) Volume 2 – June 10
Apostle
   (Hebrews 3:1-2) Volume 1 - April 24
Apostle and High Priest of our Profession
   (Hebrews 3:1) Volume 1 - September 21
Appears in the Presence of God for Us
   (Hebrews 9:24) Volume 2 – February 28
Arrow Shall go forth as the Lightning
   (Zechariah 9:14) Volume 2 – May 6
Author
   (Moroni 6:4) Volume 1 - October 25
Author and Finisher of our Faith
   (Hebrews 12:2) Volume 1 - April 16
Author of Eternal Salvation
   (Hebrews 5:9) Volume 1 - August 27

B
Bare our Sins in His Own Body
   (1 Peter 2:24) Volume 1 - November 13
Beginning and the End
   (Revelation 22:13) Volume 1 - February 23
Beginning of the Creation of God
   (Revelation 3:14) Volume 2 – March 21
Begotten of the Father
   (John 1:14) Volume 2 – March 28
Beloved and Chosen from the Beginning
   (Moses 4:2) Volume 1 - October 30
Beloved Son
   (2 Nephi 31:11) Volume 2 – March 29
Beloved Son of God
   (Matthew 3:17) Volume 1 - March 2
Beside Him there is no Savior
   (Doctrine & Covenants 76:1) Volume 3 – October 8

Better than the Angels
    (Hebrews 1:4) Volume 1 - August 10
Bishop of your Souls
    (2 Peter 2:25) Volume 1 - July 29
Blessed for Evermore
    (2 Corinthians 11:31) Volume 1 - October 1
Blessed God
    (Alma 19:29) Volume 2 – June 22
Blessed Jesus
    (Alma 19:29) Volume 2 – June 23
Blessed of God
    (Psalms 45:2) Volume 1 - September 5
Blood of Jesus Christ Cleanseth us from all Sin
    (1 John 1:7) Volume 2 – April 11
Born of a Woman
    (Alma 19:13) Volume 2 – June 24
Branch
    (Isaiah 11:1) Volume 1 - July 25
Branch of the Lord
    (2 Nephi 14:2) Volume 2 – June 25
Brazen Serpent
    (Helaman 8:14) Volume 1 - January 23
Bread of God
    (John 6:33) Volume 3 – May 31
Bread of Life
    (John 6:35) Volume 1 - January 18
Bread Which came Down from Heaven
    (John 6:41) Volume 3 – June 1
Bridegroom
    (Matthew 9:15) Volume 1 - March 20
Bright and Morning Star
    (Revelation 22:16) Volume 1 - April 6
Brightness of God's Glory
    (Hebrews 1:3) Volume 1 - February 5
Builder
    (Hebrews 11:10) Volume 3 – January 4
By Himself Purged our Sins
    (Hebrews 1:3) Volume 1 - June 28
By Whom God Made the Worlds
    (Hebrews 1:2) Volume 2 – April 12

C

Called us to Honor
(2 Peter 1:3) Volume 3 - November 26

Called us to Virtue
(2 Peter 1:3) Volume 3 – November 27

Called the Son of God, Because He Received not of the Fulness at the First
(Doctrine & Covenants 93:14) Volume 3 – June 19

Came by Water and Blood
(1 John 5:6) Volume 1 - May 15

Came down from Heaven
(John 6:51) Volume 3 – December 18

Came into the World to Save Sinners
(1 Timothy 1:15) Volume 1 - March 18

Cannot be Touched with the Feelings of our Infirmities
(Hebrews 4:15) Volume 3 – December 5

Captain
(2 Chronicles 13:12) Volume 1 - September 2

Captain of [their] Salvation
(Hebrews 2:10) Volume 1 - October 24

Carpenter
(Mark 6:3) Volume 1 - January 17

Carpenter's Son
(Matthew 13:55) Volume 1 - November 6

Causeth the Vapours to Ascend from the Ends of the Earth; He Maketh Lightnings with Rain, and Bringeth forth the Wind
(Jeremiah 10:13) Volume 3 – June 15

Chief Cornerstone
(Ephesians 2:20) Volume 1 - November 26

Chief Shepherd
(1 Peter 5:4) Volume 1 - December 6

Child
(2 Nephi 19:6) Volume 2 – December 27

Chosen of God
(John 23:35) Volume 1 - March 27

Chosen of God and Precious
(1 Peter 2:4) Volume 2 – April 9

Christ
(1 John 5:1) Volume 1 - December 4

Christ a King
(Luke 23:2) Volume 3 – March 30

Christ - For so Shall He be Called
(Mosiah 15:21) Volume 2 - June 27

Christ for their Shepherd
(Mormon 5:17) Volume 2 – October 27
Christ in God
(Doctrine & Covenants 86:9) Volume 3 – June 20
Christ Jesus
(Romans 3:24) Volume 1 – September 1
Christ of God
(John 9:20) Volume 1 – October 3
Christ, the Chosen of God
(Luke 23:35) Volume 1 – March 19
Christ, the Eternal God
(2 Nephi 26:12) Volume 2 – January 7
Christ the King of Israel
(Mark 15:32) Volume 3 – May 20
Christ the Lamb
(Doctrine & Covenants 76:85) Volume 1 – June 4
Christ the Lord
(Mosiah 16:15) Volume 2 – June 29
Christ, the Lord God Omnipotent
(Mosiah 5:15) Volume 2 – June 28
Christ the Lord, Who is the Very Eternal Father
(Mosiah 16:15) Volume 3 – August 17
Christ, the Power of God and the Wisdom of God
(1 Corinthians 1:24) Volume 2 – January 20
Christ, the Savior of the World
(John 4:42) Volume 3 – June 6
Christ the Son
(Alma 11:44) Volume 2 – June 30
Christ, the Son of the Blessed
(Mark 14:61) Volume 3 – January 12
Christ, the Son of the Living God
(Matthew 16:16) Volume 1 – December 19
Christ, Who has Broken the Bands of Death
(Mosiah 15:23) Volume 2 – July 1
Christ, Who is our Life
(Colossians 3:4) Volume 1 – December 14
Christ, Who was before the World Began
(3 Nephi 26:5) Volume 2 – October 26
Christ your Redeemer
(Moroni 8:8) Volume 3 – December 1
Cometh in an Hour you Think Not
(Doctrine & Covenants 51:20) Volume 3 – September 29
Cometh Quickly
(Doctrine & Covenants 51:20) Volume 3 – September 28

Condescension of God
(1 Nephi 11:26) Volume 2 - July 2
Confidence of all the Ends of the Earth
(Psalms 65:5) Volume 2 - June 7
Consecrated for Evermore
(Hebrews 7:28) Volume 1 - November 30
Consolation of Israel
(Luke 2:25) Volume 1 - March 10
Controllest and Subjectest the Devil, and the Dark and Benighted Dominion of Sheol
(Doctrine & Covenants 121:4) Volume 3 - June 21
Counsellor
(Isaiah 9:6) Volume 1 - January 15
Counselor
(2 Nephi 18:6) Volume 1 - June 11
Counted Worthy of More Glory than Moses
(Hebrews 3:3) Volume 1 - February 21
Course is One Eternal Round
(Doctrine & Covenants 35:1) Volume 3 - October 15
Created the Heavens and the Earth
(Doctrine & Covenants 14:9) Volume 3 - September 25
Creator
(1 Peter 4:19) Volume 1 - May 2
Creator of all Things from the Beginning
(Mosiah 3:8) Volume 3 - March 20
Creator of Heaven and Earth
(Jacob 2:5) Volume 1 - September 29
Creator of Israel
(Isaiah 43:15) Volume 1 - April 4
Creator of the Ends of the Earth
(Isaiah 40:28) Volume 1 - February 4
Creator of the First Day, the Beginning and the End
(Doctrine & Covenants 95:7) Volume 3 - March 23
Crowned with Glory and Honour
(Hebrews 2:9) Volume 1 - September 3
Crucified for the Sins of the World
(Doctrine & Covenants 54:1) Volume 3 - September 22

D
Delight to Honor those who Serve me in Righteousness and in Truth unto the End
(Doctrine & Covenants 76:5) Volume 3 - October 27
Deliverer
(Romans 11:16) Volume 1 - September 20

Deliverer from Death
   (Doctrine & Covenants 138:33) Volume 3 – October 19
Delivereth us from the Wrath to Come
   (1 Thessalonians 1:10) Volume 2 - February 29
Did no Sin
   (1 Peter 2:22) Volume 1 - May 9
Died and Rose Again
   (1 Thessalonians 4:14) Volume 1 - April 9
Door
   (John 10:9) Volume 3 – July 18
Door of the Sheep
   (John 10:7) Volume 1 - October 21

E
El
   (Bible Dictionary, p. 661) Volume 2 – June 12
El-elohe-Israel
   (Genesis 33:20) Volume 2 - April 18
Elohim
   (Bible Dictionary, p. 661) Volume 2 - May 22
Emmanuel
   (Matthew 1:23) Volume 1 - July 19
End of the Law for Righteousness
   (Romans 10:4) Volume 1 - June 17
Endless and Eternal is My Name
   (Moses 7:35) Volume 2 - April 8
Endless is My Name
   (Moses 1:3) Volume 3 – July 13
Established the World by His Wisdom
   (Jeremiah 10:12) Volume 3 – December 8
Eternal Father
   (Doctrine & Covenants 20:77) Volume 2 - February 13
Eternal Father of Heaven
   (Mormon 6:22) Volume 2 - October 29
Eternal Father of Heaven and Earth
   (Mosiah 15:4) Volume 2 - February 8
Eternal God
   (Doctrine & Covenants 121:32) Volume 2 - February 2
Eternal God, and the Messiah who is the Lamb of God
   (1 Nephi 12:18) Volume 3 – May 26
Eternal Head
   (Helaman 13:38) Volume 3 – August 29

Eternal is My Name
  (Moses 7:35) Volume 3 – August 22
Eternal Judge of Both Quick and Dead
  (Moroni 10:34) Volume 2 – February 7
Eternal King
  (Doctrine & Covenants 128:23) Volume 2 – December 28
Eternal Life
  (1 John 5:11) Volume 1 - June 13
Eternal Redemption for Us
  (Hebrews 9:12) Volume 2 - April 16
Ever Liveth to Make Intercession
  (Hebrews 7:25) Volume 2 - March 3
Everlasting Father
  (Isaiah 9:6) Volume 2 - March 1
Everlasting God, the Lord, the Creator of the Ends of the Earth
  (Isaiah 40:28) Volume 1 - January 6
Everlasting King
  (Jeremiah 10:10) Volume 3 – July 23
Everlasting Light
  (Isaiah 60:19) Volume 1 - October 18
Ever Liveth to Make Intercession
  (Hebrews 7:25) Volume 2 - March 3
Example
  (John 13:15) Volume 1 - February 27
Example of the Son
  (2 Nephi 31:16) Volume 1 - June 10
Excellent is Thy Name
  (Psalms 8:1) Volume 1 - January 28
Express Image of God's Person
  (Hebrews 1:3) Volume 1 - December 24

F
Faithful
  (1 Corinthians 10:13) Volume 1 - December 17
Faithful and Just
  (1 John 1:9) Volume 1 - December 16
Faithful and True
  (Revelation 19:11) Volume 1 - May 11
Faithful Creator
  (1 Peter 4:19) Volume 3 – March 18
Faithful Witness
  (Revelation 1:5) Volume 1 - May 28

Faithfulness [is] the Girdle of His Reins
   (Isaiah 11:5) Volume 1 - December 15
Father
   (Acts 1:4) Volume 1 - June 22
Father and I are One
   (3 Nephi 28:10) Volume 2 – February 4
Father also Which is in Heaven
   (Mark 11:2) Volume 3 – July 12
Father and the Son
   (2 John 1:9) Volume 1 - November 15
Father, and the Son, and the Holy Ghost
   (3 Nephi 11:27) Volume 2 - February 3
Father, even the Spirit of Truth
   (John 15:26) Volume 3 – April 5
Father is in Me
    (3 Nephi 9:15) Volume 3 – September 15
Father, Lord of Heaven and Earth
   (Luke 10:21) Volume 3 – April 8
Father of All
   (Ephesians 4:6) Volume 3 – July 29
Father of all Things
   (Mosiah 7:27) Volume 2 - July 3
Father of Circumcision
   (Romans 4:12) Volume 3 - April 7
Father of Glory
   (Ephesians 1:17) Volume 3 – January 16
Father of Heaven and Earth
   (Mosiah 3:8) Volume 3 – July 19
Father of Heaven and of Earth
   (2 Nephi 25:12) Volume 1 - March 28
Father of Lights
   (James 1:17) Volume 1 - January 26
Father of Mercies
   (2 Corinthians 1:3) Volume 3 – March 27
Father of our Lord Jesus Christ
    (2 Corinthians 1:3) Volume 3 – April 12
Father of Spirits
   (Hebrews 12:9) Volume 1 - November 7
Father of the Heavens and of the Earth, and all Things that in them Are
   (Ether 4:7) Volume 2 – November 4
Father of us All
   (Romans 4:16) Volume 3 – May 10
Father, Son, and Holy Ghost are One God, Infinite and Eternal, without End
   (Doctrine & Covenants 20:28) Volume 3 – June 23

Father which is in Heaven
   (Matthew 10:33) Volume 3 – March 2
Fear of God
   (Genesis 20:11) Volume 1 - January 4
Fear of Isaac
   (Genesis 31:42) Volume 2 – April 2
Fellowservant
   (Revelation 22:9) Volume 1 - May 29
Figure for the Time then Present
   (Hebrews 9:9) Volume 2 - January 14
Finisher of their Faith
   (Moroni 6:4) Volume 2 – November 12
Fire
   (2 Nephi 20:17) Volume 2 - July 4
First and the Last
   (Isaiah 44:6) Volume 1 - January 31
First Begotten
   (Hebrews 1:6) Volume 1 - February 19
First Begotten of the Dead
   (Revelation 1:5) Volume 1 - October 22
Firstborn
   (Romans 8:29) Volume 1 - May 4
Firstborn from the Dead
   (Colossians 1:18) Volume 3 – August 23
Firstborn Son
   (Matthew 1:25) Volume 3 – December 20
First Fruits
   (Doctrine & Covenants 88:98) Volume 3 – June 24
Firstfruits of them that Slept
   (1 Corinthians 15:20) Volume 1 - December 29
Firstfruits unto God
   (2 Nephi 2:9) Volume 3 – January 1
Flame
   (2 Nephi 20:17) Volume 2 – July 5
Foreordained Before the Foundation of the World
   (1 Peter 1:20) Volume 1 – July 2
Forerunner
   (Hebrews 6:20) Volume 1 - August 13
Formed thee from the Womb
   (Isaiah 44:24) Volume 3 – December 24
Foundation of the Church
   (1 Corinthians 3:11) Volume 1 – July 20
Founder of Peace
   (Mosiah 15:18) Volume 2 - November 21

Fountain of Living Waters
    (Jeremiah 2:13) Volume 1 - July 3
Fountain of the Water of Life
    (Revelation 21:6) Volume 1 - December 11
Framer of Heaven and Earth, and all Things which are in Them
    (Doctrine & Covenants 20:17) Volume 2 - December 20
From all Eternity to all Eternity
    (Moroni 8:18) Volume 3 – November 21
From Everlasting to Everlasting
    (Doctrine & Covenants 20:17) Volume 2 - November 30
Full of Equity
    (Alma 9:26) Volume 3 – December 26
Full of Grace
    (Alma 9:26) Volume 3 – October 31
Full of Grace and Truth
    (2 Nephi 2:6) Volume 2 - July 6
Full of Mercy
    (Alma 9:26) Volume 3 – November 4
Full of Patience
    (Alma 9:26) Volume 3 – November 3
Full of Truth
    (Alma 9:26) Volume 3 – November 2

G
Gave Himself for our Sins
    (Galatians 1:4) Volume 1 - January 8
Gave Himself for Us
    (Titus 2:14) Volume 1 - March 5
Gift of God
    (John 4:10) Volume 3 – June 5
Gift of His Son
    (Ether 12:11) Volume 2 - November 10
Given us Understanding that We May Know Him that is True
    (1 John 5:20) Volume 1 - August 20
Giveth Life to all Things
    (Doctrine & Covenants 88:13) Volume 3 – October 5
Giveth you Light
    (Doctrine & Covenants 88:11) Volume 3 – October 7
Glory and Virtue
    (2 Peter 1:3) Volume 2 - January 27
Glory of the God of Israel
    (Ezekiel 9:3) Volume 1 – May 30

Glory of the Lord
   (Ezekiel 1:28) Volume 3 – December 14
God
   (Malachi 1:11) Volume 1 - May 20
God an High Priest after the Order of Melchisedec
   (Hebrews 5:10) Volume 3 – January 10
God and Christ are the Judge of All
   (Doctrine & Covenants 76:68) Volume 3 – June 26
God and Father of our Lord Jesus Christ
   (1 Peter 1:3) Volume 1 - August 19
God and His Father
   (Revelation 1:6) Volume 1 – May 31
God and my Savior
   (3 Nephi 5:20) Volume 3 – October 24
God and our Father
   (Galatians 1:4) Volume 3 – April 24
God and Rock of their Salvation
   (Jacob 7:25) Volume 2 - July 7
God and the Father
   (James 1:27) Volume 1 - June 1
God and the Father of our Lord Jesus Christ
   (Colossians 1:3) Volume 2 - April 10
God and the Lamb
   (Doctrine & Covenants 76:119) Volume 3 – January 2
God, Even our Father
   (1 Thessalonians 3:13) Volume 3 – March 1
God, even the Father
   (James 3:9) Volume 3 – March 16
God in Heaven
   (Joseph Smith Matthew 1:40) Volume 3 – March 4
God in Heaven, Who is Infinite and Eternal
   (Doctrine & Covenants 20:17) Volume 3 – June 27
God in the Highest
   (Luke 2:14) Volume 2 - January 29
God is Judge Himself
   (Psalms 50:6) Volume 3 – March 25
God is Light
   (1 John 5:3) Volume 3- February 6
God is Love
   (1 John 4:8) Volume 1 - April 25
God is Merciful
   (Doctrine & Covenants 2:10) Volume 2 – December 1
God is Mindful of every People
   (Alma 26:37) Volume 2 - July 8

God is with Us
　(Alma 56:46) Volume 2 - July 9
God is with Thee in all that Thou Doest
　(Genesis 21:22) Volume 3 – November 20
God is with You
　(Zechariah 8:23) Volume 3 – December 6
God Manifest in the Flesh
　(1 Timothy 3:16) Volume 2 - March 2
God of Abraham, the God of Isaac, the God of Jacob
　(Exodus 3:6) Volume 1 - May 27
God of all Comfort
　(2 Corinthians 1:3) Volume 3 – March 28
God of Beth-el
　(Genesis 31:13) Volume 1 - February 28
God of Glory
　(Moses 1:20) Volume 2 - January 9
God of Gods
　(Deuteronomy 10:176) Volume 2 - January 28
God of Heaven
　(Moses 7:28) Volume 2 -   February 10
God of Israel
　(2 Nephi 25:14) Volume 1 - March 24
God of Israel Shall be your Rearward
　(3 Nephi 20:42) Volume 2 - October 21
God of Israel, Who is the Lord of Hosts
　(1 Nephi 20:2) Volume 2 - July 10
God of Jeshurun
　(Deuteronomy 33:26) Volume 3 – March 3
God of Knowledge
　(1 Samuel 2:3) Volume 1 - December 12
God of Miracles
　(2 Nephi 28:6) Volume 2 – July 11
God of my Rock, my Shield, and the Horn of my Salvation, my High Tower, and my Refuge, my Savior
　(2 Samuel 22:3) Volume 1 - July 5
God of my Salvation
　(Psalms 18:46) Volume 1 - February 2
God of Nature
　(1 Nephi 18:12) Volume 2 – July 12
God of our Fathers
　(1 Nephi 19:10) Volume 2 – July 13
God of our Lord Jesus Christ, the Father of Glory
　(Ephesians 1:17) Volume 3 – May 9

God of our Salvation
(Psalms 65:5) Volume 2 - November 3
God of the Hebrews
(Exodus 5:3) Volume 1 - August 25
God of the Whole Earth
(Isaiah 54:5) Volume 1 - June 2
God of this People Israel
(Acts 13:17) Volume 2 - February 11
God of thy Father
(Genesis 46:3) Volume 1 – May 26
God our Father
(1 Thessalonians 1:1) Volume 3 – April 2
God our Father and Jesus Christ our Lord
(2 Timothy 1:2) Volume 2 – April 27
God our Father and the Lord Jesus Christ
(Romans 1:7) Volume 1 - July 21
God our Savior
(Jude 1:25) Volume 1 - June 27
God over all the Earth
(1 Nephi 11:6) Volume 1 - September 26
God the Eternal Father
(Doctrine & Covenants 20:77) Volume 2 – January 5
God the Father
(Jude 1:1) Volume 1 - December 21
God the Father and Christ Jesus our Lord
(2 Timothy 1:2) Volume 3 – March 14
God the Father and His Only Begotten Son, Jesus Christ
(Doctrine & Covenants 138:14) Volume 3 – June 28
God the Father and the Lord Jesus Christ our Saviour
(Titus 1:4) Volume 2 – April 13
God, the Greatest of All
(Doctrine & Covenants 19:18) Volume 1 - February 15
God the Judge of All
(Hebrews 12:23) Volume 1 - March 11
God Who Brought the Children of Israel out of the Land of Egypt
(Mosiah 7:19) Volume 2 – September 29
God Who was the God of Abraham, and Isaac, and Jacob
(Mosiah 7:19) Volume 2 – September 29
God will Deliver Us
(Alma 58:37) Volume 2 - July 14
God with Us
(Matthew 1:23) Volume 3 – June 14
God's Anointed
(Acts 4:27) Volume 1 - March 25

God's Holy Child Jesus
 (Acts 4:27) Volume 1 - December 27
Good
 (Psalms 34:8) Volume 1 - April 22
Good Shepherd
 (John 10:14) Volume 1 - May 13
Good unto Them that Wait for Him
 (Lamentations 3:25) Volume 3 – November 11
Governor that Shall Rule Israel
 (Matthew 2:6) Volume 1 - July 27
Gracious
 (Doctrine & Covenants 76:5) Volume 3 – December 13
Gracious and Merciful, Slow to Anger, and of Great Kindness
 (Joel 2:13) Volume 3 – November 30
Granted Salvation unto His People
 (Mosiah 15:18) Volume 2 - February 15
Great and Eternal Head
 (Helaman 13:38) Volume 2 - October 8
Great and True Shepherd
 (Helaman 15:13) Volume 1 - June 26
Great Creator
 (Jacob 3:7) Volume 1 - August 22
Great God
 (Titus 2:13) Volume 1 - April 14
Great God and a Great King
 (Psalms 95:3) Volume 1 - November 29
Great...Head
 (Helaman 13:38) Volume 3 – August 28
Great High Priest, that is Passed into the Heavens
 (Hebrews 4:14) Volume 2 - December 30
Great I Am, Alpha and Omega, the Beginning and the End
 (Doctrine & Covenants 36:1) Volume 3 – October 18
Great I Am, even Jesus Christ
 (Doctrine & Covenants 39:1) Volume 3 – June 29
Great Jehovah
 (Doctrine & Covenants 128:9) Volume 1 - March 30
Great Jehovah, the Eternal Judge of Both Quick and Dead
 (Moroni 10:64) Volume 3 – January 15
Great King
 (Malachi 1:14) Volume 1 - January 19
Great Light
 (Matthew 4:16) Volume 1 - December 9
Great Mediator
 (2 Nephi 2:28) Volume 2 - July 15

Great Mediator of all Men
   (2 Nephi 2:27) Volume 2 – January 13
Great Shepherd of the Sheep
   (Hebrews 13:20) Volume 1 - May 14
[A] Great Spirit
   (Alma 18:26) Volume 2 - July 16
[The] Great Spirit
   (Alma 18:3) Volume 2 – July 17
[This] Great Spirit, Who is God
   (Alma 18:28) Volume 2 - July 18
[That] Great Spirit, Who knows all Things
   (Alma 18:18) Volume 2 - July 19
Great, the Mighty God, Lord of Hosts, is His Name
   (Jeremiah 32:18) Volume 3 – October 26

H
Hand of the Lord
   (Ruth 1:13) Volume 3 – December 17
Hath an Unchangeable Priesthood
   (Hebrews 7:24) Volume 2 - April 14
Hath given us Understanding that we may Know Him that is True
   (1 John 5:20) Volume 2 - April 15
He Hath made the Earth by His Power
   (Jeremiah 51:15) Volume 3 – August 16
He is a Man like Ourselves
   (Doctrine & Covenants 129:1) Volume 2 – December 12
He is Above all Things, and In all Things, and is Through all Things, and is Round About all Things
   (Doctrine & Covenants 88:41) Volume 2 - April 17
He is an Holy God; He is a Jealous God
   (Joshua 24:19) Volume 3 – February 26
He is Full of Mercy, Justice, Grace and Truth, and Peace
   (Doctrine & Covenants 84:102) Volume 3 – June 25
He is Harmless
   (Hebrews 7:26 Volume 3 – September 9
He is in the Moon
   (Doctrine & Covenants 88:8) Volume 3 – August 31
He is in the Sun
   (Doctrine & Covenants 88:7) Volume 3 – September 3
He is Pure
   (Moroni 7:48) Volume 2 - November 16
He is the Light of the Moon
   (Doctrine & Covenants 88:8) Volume 3 – September 1

He is the Light of the Sun
    (Doctrine & Covenants 88:7) Volume 3 - September 4
He is the Power thereof by which (the Moon) was Made
    (Doctrine & Covenants 88:8) Volume 3 - September 2
He is the Power thereof by which (the Sun) was Made
    (Doctrine & Covenants 88:7) Volume 3 - September 5
He is the Same, and His Years never Fail
    (Doctrine & Covenants 76:4) Volume 2 - December 14
He Shall be Called by the Name of Christ
    (Mosiah 5:9) Volume 2 - July 20
He Shall be Called the Lord our Righteousness
    (Jeremiah 23:6) Volume 3 - December 15
He Shall be Called the Son of God
    (Mosiah 15:2) Volume 2 - July 21
He that Ascended up on High
    (Doctrine & Covenants 88:6) Volume 3 - June 30
He that Cometh in the Name of the Lord
    (Matthew 21:9) Volume 2 - March 5
He That Formed Thee from the Womb
    (Isaiah 44:24) Volume 3 - January 23
He that Giveth Salvation unto Kings
    (Psalms 144:10) Volume 2 - April 28
He that Hath Cut Rahab
    (2 Nephi 8:9) Volume 2 - July 22
He that Hath the Key of David
    (Revelation 3:7) Volume 2 - April 21
He that is Born King of the Jews
    (Matthew 2:2) Volume 3 - December 21
He that is Holy
    (Revelation 3:7) Volume 2 - March 6
He was called the Son of God, Because He Received not of the Fulness at the First
    (Doctrine & Covenants 93:14) Volume 3 - June 19
He was in the Beginning, Before the World Was
    (Doctrine & Covenants 93:7) Volume 2 - April 19
He Who came unto His Own
    (Doctrine & Covenants 88:48) Volume 2 - April 22
He Who Controllest and Subjectest the Devil, and the Dark and Benighted Dominion of Sheol
    (Doctrine & Covenants 121:4) Volume 3 - June 21
He Who hath dried the Sea
    (2 Nephi 8:10) Volume 3 - July 4
He Who was Crucified for the Sins of the World
    (Doctrine & Covenants 54:1) Volume 3 - June 22

Head of Every Man
(1 Corinthians 11:3) Volume 3 – September 6
Head of the Body
(Colossians 1:18) Volume 1 - December 18
Head of the Church
(Ephesians 5:23) Volume 1 - May 12
Head of the Corner
(1 Peter 2:7) Volume 2 – February 12
Head Stone of the Corner
(Psalms 118:22) Volume 1 - October 15
Healeth the People
(2 Chronicles 3:20) Volume 1 - February 12
Heavenly Father
(Matthew 15:13) Volume 3 – October 17
Heavenly King
(Mosiah 2:19) Volume 1 – September 8
Heir of all Things
(Hebrews 1:2) Volume 1 – December 5
High and Lofty One that Inhabits Eternity
(Isaiah 57:15) Volume 1 - April 2
High Calling of God
(Philippians 3:14) Volume 1 - September 11
The High God
(Micah 6:6) Volume 3 – August 13
High God their Redeemer
(Psalms 78:35) Volume 3 – January 31
High Priest
(Hebrews 4:15) Volume 3 – December 6
High Priest after the Order of Melchizedek
(Hebrews 5:10) Volume 1 - May 16
High Priest For Ever after the Order of Melchisedec
(Hebrews 6:20) Volume 3 – January 7
High Priest of Good Things to Come
(Hebrews 9:11) Volume 1 - October 2
High Priest Which Cannot be Touched with the Feelings of our Infirmities
(Hebrews 4:15) Volume 3 – January 13
High Priest Who is Set on the Right Hand of the Throne of the Majesty in the Heavens
(Hebrews 8:1) Volume 3 – January 14
Highest
(Luke 1:35) Volume 3 – January 9
Highest of All
(Doctrine & Covenants 76:70) Volume 1 - October 6
Him that Bringeth Good Tidings
(Mosiah 15:18) Volume 2 – July 23

Him that Hath called us to Glory and Virtue
  (2 Peter 1:3) Volume 2 – January 27
Him that is True
  (1 John 5:20) Volume 2 – April 23
Him Who has all Power
  (Doctrine & Covenants 61:1) Volume 3 – July 1
Him Who has Ordained you from on High
  (Doctrine & Covenants 77:2) Volume 2 – December 3
Him Who is from all Eternity to all Eternity
  (Doctrine & Covenants 39:1) Volume 3 – July 2
His Holy Child, Jesus
  (Moroni 8:3) Volume 2 – November 17
His Holy Will
  (Moroni 7:2) Volume 2 – November 13
His Son, Jesus Christ
  (Moroni 7:48) Volume 2 – November 15
His Word
  (2 Nephi 19:8) Volume 2 – July 24
His Years Never Fail
  (Doctrine & Covenants 76:4) Volume 3 – September 6
Hole of the Pit from Whence ye are Digged
  (2 Nephi 8:1) Volume 3 – April 16
Holiest of All
  (Hebrews 9:3) Volume 1 - September 28
Holiness of Jesus Christ
  (Mormon 9:5) Volume 2 – October 31
Holiness unto the Lord
  (Zechariah 14:20) Volume 3 – July 25
Holy
  (Hebrews 7:26) Volume 3 – September 8
Holy Child
  (Moroni 8:3) Volume 1 - December 25
Holy Child, Jesus
  (Moroni 8:3) Volume 2 – November 17
Holy Father
  (John 17:11) Volume 3 – April 30
Holy God
  (2 Nephi 9:39) Volume 2 – July 25
Holy, Harmess [and] Undefiled, Separate from Sinners, and Made Higher than the Heavens
  (Hebrews 7:26) Volume 2 – March 8
Holy, Holy God
  (Alma 31:15) Volume 2 – July 26

Holy, Holy, Holy
(Isaiah 6:3) Volume 1 - February 9
Holy, Holy, Holy is the Lord of Hosts
(2 Nephi 16:3) Volume 3 - February 19
Holy Messiah
(2 Nephi 2:6) Volume 2 - April 4
Holy One
(Isaiah 43:15) Volume 2 - March 7
Holy One and the Just
(Acts 3:14) Volume 1 - October 20
Holy One of God
(Mark 1:24) Volume 3 - February 7
Holy One of Israel
(Isaiah 1:4) Volume 1 - June 20
Holy One of Israel, the True Messiah, their Redeemer and their God
(2 Nephi 1:10) Volume 3 - February 16
Holy One, the Creator of Israel
(Isaiah 43:15) Volume 1 - August 18
Hope of Glory
(Colossians 1:27) Volume 2 - March 9
Hope of His People
(Joel 3:16) Volume 1 - October 8
Hope of Israel
(Acts 28:20) Volume 1 - February 22
Horn of David
(Psalms 132:17) Volume 2 - June 9
Horn of my Salvation
(2 Samuel 22:3) Volume 3 - July 15
Hosanna in the Highest
(Mark 11:10) Volume 3 - January 11

I
I Am
(John 8:58) Volume 1 - September 12
I am a God of Miracles
(2 Nephi 27:23) Volume 2 - July 27
I am also the Last
(1 Nephi 20:12) Volume 3 - September 13
I am Come in My Father's Name
(John 5:43) Volume 3 - March 9
I am God
(Moses 7:35) Volume 2 - January 19

I am He
   (John 18:5) Volume 3 – September 11
I am He; I am the First, and I am also the Last
   (1 Nephi 20:12) Volume 2 - July 31
I am He of whom Moses Spake
   (3 Nephi 20:23) Volume 2 – October 20
I am He that Comforteth You
   (2 Nephi 8:12) Volume 2 - July 28
I am He that Gave the Law
   (3 Nephi 15:5) Volume 2 - October 16
I am He, the Beginning and the End, the Redeemer of the World
   (Doctrine & Covenants 19:1) Volume 3 – June 18
I am He who Covenanted with my People Israel
   (3 Nephi 15:5) Volume 2 – October 17
I am He who Liveth
   (Doctrine & Covenants 110:4) Volume 3 – July 3
I am He Who said—Other Sheep have I Which are not of this Fold
   (Doctrine & Covenants 10:59) Volume 2 - November 29
I am He Who spake in Righteousness
   (Doctrine & Covenants 133:47) Volume 2 – December 2
I am He Who Speaketh
   (Ether 4:8) Volume 2 - November 5
I am He Who was Slain
   (Doctrine & Covenants 110:4) Volume 2 - December 4
I am in the Father, and the Father in Me
   (3 Nephi 9:15) Volume 2 – October 11
I am Jesus Christ
   (Doctrine & Covenants 51:20) Volume 3 – September 27
I am Jesus Christ the Son of God
   (Doctrine & Covenants 35:2) Volume 3 – April 11
I am Jesus Christ, the Son of God, Who was Crucified for the Sins of the World
   (Doctrine & Covenants 35:2) Volume 2 – August 2
I am Jesus Christ the Son of the Living God
   (Doctrine & Covenants 14:9) Volume 3 – September 24
I am Jesus Christ, Who Cometh Quickly, in an Hour you Think Not
   (Doctrine & Covenants 51:20) Volume 2 - August 6
I am no Respecter of Pesons
   (Doctrine & Covenants 1:35) Volume 3 – July 11
I am not of this World
   (John 17:16) Volume 3 – June 10
I am One in the Father
   (Doctrine & Covenants 35:2) Volume 3 – May 16
I am That I am
   (Exodus 3:14) Volume 1 - November 3

I am the Almighty God
   (Genesis 17:1) Volume 3 – November 7
I am the Door
   (John 10:9) Volume 3 – June 2
I am the Father
   (Ether 4:12) Volume 2 – November 6
I am the Father and the Son
   (Ether 3:14) Volume 2 – April 26
I am the First
   (1 Nephi 20:12) Volume 3 – September 12
I am the Firstborn
   (Doctrine & Covenants 93:21) Volume 3 – September 21
I am the God of Israel
   (3 Nephi 11:14) Volume 3 – September 17
I am the God of the Whole Earth
   (3 Nephi 11:14) Volume 3 – September 18
I am the God of thy Fathers, the God of Abraham, the God of Isaac, and the God of Jacob
   (Acts 7:32) Volume 3 – May 3
I am the Law, and the Light
   (3 Nephi 15:9) Volume 1 – May 17
I am the Life and the Light of the World
   (Doctrine & Covenants 11:28) Volume 2 – December 6
I am the Light of the World
   (Doctrine & Covenants 11:28) Volume 3 – October 22
I am the Light which ye shall Hold Up
   (3 Nephi 18:24) Volume 2 – October 19
I am the Lord
   (Ezekiel 6:7) Volume 3 – September 19
I am the Lord, the God of all Flesh
   (Jeremiah 32:27) Volume 3 – August 15
I am the Lord thy God
   (2 Nephi 8:16) Volume 2 – April 24
I am the Lord thy God from the land of Egypt
   (Hosea 13:4) Volume 3 – May 14
I am the Lord your God dwelling in Zion, My Holy Mountain
   (Joel 3:17) Volume 2 – August 7
I am the Root and the Offspring of David
   (Revelation 22:16) Volume 3 – May 17
I am the Same that Came unto Mine Own, and Mine Own Received Me Not
   (Doctrine & Covenants 6:21) Volume 3 – January 6
I am the Same that Leadeth Men to all Good
   (Ether 4:12) Volume 2 – November 7

I am the Son
   (Ether 3:14) Volume 3 – September 16
I am the True Light that is in You
   (Doctrine & Covenants 88:50) Volume 2 – April 25
I am the True Light that Lighteth every Man that Cometh into the World
   (Doctrine & Covenants 93:2) Volume 2 – November 26
I am their Redeemer
   (Mosiah 26:26) Volume 3 – December 16
I am with the Faithful Always
   (Doctrine & Covenants 62:9) Volume 2 – November 27
I am your Sign
   (Ezekiel 12:11) Volume 3 – September 4
I, and the Holy Ghost are One
   (3 Nephi 11:36) Volume 2 – October 14
I bear record of the Father
   (3 Nephi 11:32) Volume 2 – October 13
I, God
   (Doctrine & Covenants 19:16) Volume 2 – January 18
I, Jesus Christ, your Lord and your God, and your Redeemer
   (Doctrine & Covenants 18:47) Volume 2 – August 9
I that Am the Lord thy God
   (Hosea 12:9) Volume 3 – November 15
I, the Lord
   (1 Nephi 20:15) Volume 2 – August 3
I, the Lord, am Merciful
   (Doctrine & Covenants 70:18) Volume 2 – December 5
I, the Lord, am Merciful and Gracious unto Those who Fear Me, and Delight to Honor those who Serve me in Righteousness and in Truth unto the End
   (Doctrine & Covenants 76:5) Volume 2 – August 27
I the Lord am thy God
   (Doctrine & Covenants 132:47) Volume 3 – May 11
I the Lord am thy Savior and thy Redeemer
   (2 Nephi 6:18) Volume 3 – September 20
I The Lord am thy Savior and thy Redeemer, the Mighty One of Jacob
   (Isaiah 60:16) Volume 3 – February 3
I the Lord God
   (Doctrine & Covenants 34:1) Volume 2 – January 23
I the Lord thy God am a Jealous God
   (Mosiah 13:13) Volume 2 – July 29
I was in the Beginning with the Father
   (Doctrine & Covenants 93:21) Volume 3 – November 5
I will be a God unto thee, and to thy seed after thee
   (Genesis 17:7) Volume 3 – December 19

I will be their God
(Ezekiel 11:20) Volume 3 – November 14

I will be unto Ephraim as a Lion, and as a Young Lion to the House of Judah
(Hosea 5:14) Volume 3 – July 24

Image of God
(2 Corinthians 4:4) Volume 1 - April 18

Immanuel
(Doctrine & Covenants 128:22) Volume 2 - March 10

In all Things
(Doctrine & Covenants 88:41) Volume 2 – April 7

In the Beginning the Word was, for He was the Word, even the Messenger of Salvation
(Doctrine & Covenants 93:8) Volume 2 – August 4

In whom is Salvation
(2 Timothy 2:10) Volume 2 – April 29

Inhabits Eternity
(Isaiah 57:15) Volume 3 – July 19

Is not the Lord in Zion?
(Jeremiah 8:19) Volume 3 – December 29

Israel's God
(Doctrine & Covenants 27:3) Volume 3 – July 30

It is I that hath Spoken it
(Ether 4:19) Volume 2 – November 9

J

JAH
(Psalms 68:3) Volume 2 – March 17

Jehovah
(Exodus 6:3) Volume 1 - October 17

Jehovah, Mighty God of Jacob
(Doctrine & Covenants 109:68) Volume 1 - October 4

Jehovah, the Eternal Judge
(Moroni 10:34) Volume 1 - April 7

Jesus
(Romans 3:26) Volume 1 - May 18

Jesus Christ
(Ephesians 2:20) Volume 1 - June 12

Jesus Christ, even the Father and the Son
(Mormon 9:12) Volume 2 – October 30

Jesus Christ His Son
(1 John 1:7) Volume 1 - May 10

Jesus Christ is the Name which is Given of the Father
(Doctrine & Covenants 18:23) Volume 3 – July 5

Jesus Christ of Nazareth
  (Acts 4:10) Volume 1 - February 10
Jesus Christ our Lord
  (2 Timothy 1:2) Volume 3 – August 26
Jesus Christ the Righteous
  (1 John 2:1) Volume 1 - April 10)
Jesus Christ, the Son of David, the Son of Abraham
  (Matthew 1:1) Volume 3 – June 12
Jesus Christ, the Son of God
  (2 Nephi 25:19) Volume 2 – August 1
Jesus Christ, the Son of God, the Father of Heaven and Earth, the Creator of all Things from the Beginning
  (Mosiah 3:8) Volume 1 – October 7
Jesus Christ, your Lord and your God
  (Doctrine & Covenants 18:47) Volume 3 – January 22
Jesus Christ, your Lord and your Redeemer
  (Doctrine & Covenants 15:1) Volume 3 – January 25
Jesus Christ, your Lord, your God, and your Redeemer
  (Doctrine & Covenants 27:1) Volume 3 – January 26
Jesus Christ, your Redeemer, the Great I Am
  (Doctrine & Covenants 29:1) Volume 3 – May 23
Jesus is the Christ
  (Moroni 7:44) Volume 2 – November 14
Jesus is the Very Christ
  (2 Nephi 26:12) Volume 2 – January 22
Jesus of Galilee
  (1 Timothy 2:5) Volume 1 - April 19
Jesus of Nazareth
  (Matthew 26:71) Volume 1 - December 1
Jesus of Nazareth the King of the Jews
  (John 19:19) Volume 3 – May 18
Jesus of Nazareth, the Son of Joseph
  (John 1:45) Volume 3 – June 8
Jesus our Lord
  (Romans 4:24) Volume 2 – March 11
Jesus, the King of the Jews
  (Matthew 27:37) Volume 3 – February 5
Jesus, the Mediator of the New Covenant
  (Doctrine & Covenants 107:19) Volume 2 – January 3
Jesus the Prophet of Nazareth of Galilee
  (Matthew 21:11) Volume 3 – December 23
Jesus the Son of God
  (Hebrews 4:14) Volume 1 - March 21

Jesus, thou Son of God
   (Alma 36:18) Volume 2 – August 10
Jesus, thou Son of God Most High
   (Luke 8:28) Volume 3 – January 17
Jesus Who is Called Christ
   (Matthew 1:16) Volume 3 – June 13
Joseph's Son
   (Luke 4:22) Volume 1 - October 27
Judge of All
   (Hebrews 12:23) Volume 2 – March 12
Judge of All the Earth
   (Genesis 18:25) Volume 1 - January 2
Judge of Both the Quick and the Dead
   (Acts 10:42) Volume 1 - August 3
The Judge of Quick and Dead
   (Acts 10:42) Volume 1 - April 20
Just God
   (Alma 29:4) Volume 2 – August 11
Just Lord
   (Zephaniah 3:5) Volume 2 – April 21
Just One
   (Acts 7:52) Volume 1 - November 20

K
Key of David
   (Revelation 3:7) Volume 1 - January 5
King
   (Isaiah 6:5) Volume 1 - March 26
King Eternal
   (1 Timothy 1:17) Volume 1 - March 7
King Immanuel
   (Doctrine & Covenants 128:22) Volume 2 – April 26
King of all the Earth
   (Psalms 47:7) Volume 1 - July 30
King of Glory
   (Psalms 24:7) Volume 2 – February 27
King of Heaven
   (2 Nephi 10:14) Volume 1 - November 8
King of Israel
   (Matthew 27:42) Volume 2 – June 13
King of Kings
   (Revelation 17:14) Volume 1 - July 26

King of Nations
   (Jeremiah 10:7) Volume 3 – December 30
King of Righteousness
   (Hebrews 7:2) Volume 3 – May 22
King of Saints
   Revelation 15:3) Volume 1 - December 7
King of Sion
   (Matthew 21:5) Volume 1 - July 6
King of the Jews
   (Matthew 2:2) Volume 1 - December 28
King of Zion
   (Moses 7:53) Volume 2 - April 6
King over All the Earth
   (Zechariah 14:9) Volume 3 – July 6
King that Cometh in the Name of the Lord
   (Luke 19:38) Volume 1 - December 30
Knew no Sin
   (2 Corinthians 5:21) Volume 1 - July 15
Knoweth the Weakness of Man
   (Doctrine & Covenants 62:1) Volume 3 – October 10

L
Lamb
   (Revelation 5:5) Volume 1 - July 8
Lamb of God, Which Taken Away the Sin of the World
   (John 1:29) Volume 3 – June 7
Lamb Slain from Before the Foundation of the World
   (Revelation 13:8) Volume 1 - April 26
Lamb that was Slain
   (Revelation 5:12) Volume 1 - June 21
Lamb without Blemish and without Spot
   (1 Peter 1:19) Volume 1 - July 31
Law, and the Life, and the Truth
   (Ether 4:12) Volume 1 - October 23
Lawgiver
   (Isaiah 33:22) Volume 1 - September 7

Lawgiver, Who is Able to Save
   (James 4:12) Volume 1 - November 17
Leadeth all Men to all Good
   (Ether 4:12) Volume 1 – October 1
Learned Obedience by the Things Which He Suffered
   (Hebrews 5:8) Volume 1 - March 3

Left us an Example
   (1 Peter 2:21) Volume 2 – April 30
Life
   (John 11:25) Volume 3 – August 6
Life of Men and the Light of Men
   (Doctrine & Covenants 93:9) Volume 2 – February 24
Life which is Endless
   (Mosiah 16:9) Volume 2 – August 12
Light
   (John 1:7) Volume 1 - November 16
Light and my Salvation
   (Psalms 27:1) Volume 2 – June 17
Light and the Life of the World
   (Doctrine & Covenants 39:2) Volume 2 – April 5
Light, and the Life, and the Truth of the World
   (Ether 4:12) Volume 1 - April 27
Light and the Redeemer of the World
   (Doctrine & Covenants 93:9) Volume 1 – November 21
Light in the Wilderness
   (1 Nephi 17:13) Volume 2 – August 13
Light into the World
   (John 12:46) Volume 3 – June 3
Light of Christ
   (Doctrine & Covenants 88:7) Volume 2 – May 1
Light of Israel
   (2 Nephi 20:17) Volume 1 - August 4
Light of Life
   (John 8:12)   Volume 1 - October 28
Light of Men
   (John 1:4) Volume 1 - March 13
Light of the Moon
   (Doctrine & Covenants 88:8) Volume 3 – September 1
Light of the Stars
   (Doctrine & Covenants 88:9) Volume 3 – October 2
Light of the World
   (John 8:12) Volume 1 - December 10
Light that is Endless
   (Mosiah 16:9) Volume 2 – June 11
Light to Lighten the Gentiles
   (Luke 2:32) Volume 1 - September 22
Light to the Gentiles
   (1 Nephi 21:6) Volume 2 – December 25
Light which Cannot be Hid in Darkness
   (Doctrine & Covenants 14:9) Volume 2 – December 7

Light which is in all Things, which Giveth Life to all Things
    (Doctrine & Covenants 88:13) Volume 2 – May 21
Light which Shineth
    (Doctrine & Covenants 88:11) Volume 3 – October 6
Light which Shineth in Darkness
    (Doctrine & Covenants 6:21) Volume 2 – February 26
Light which Shineth in Darkness and the Darkness Comprehendeth it Not
    (Doctrine & Covenants 39:2) Volume 2 – December 23
Light which Shineth, which Giveth you Light
    (Doctrine & Covenants 88:11) Volume 2 – May 2
Lighteth every Man
    (John 1:19) Volume 3 – August 12
Lighteth every Man that Cometh into the World
    (Doctrine & Covenants 93:2) Volume 3 – September 23
Like Fuller's Soap
    (Doctrine & Covenants 128:24) Volume 2 – December 8
Like unto Thee, O Lord, among the Gods
    (Exodus 15:11) Volume 1 - April 12
Lion of the Tribe of Judah
    (Revelation 5:5) Volume 2 – February 17
Liveth
    (Doctrine & Covenants 110:4) Volume 2 – February 6
Liveth and was Dead
    (Revelation 1:18) Volume 1 - December 8
Liveth For Ever and Ever
    (Revelation 4:9) Volume 2 – March 20
Living and True God
    (1 Thessalonians 1:9) Volume 1 - November 19
Living Bread
    (John 6:51) Volume 3 – July 21
Living Bread which Came Down from Heaven
    (John 6:51) Volume 1 - August 14
Living Father
    (John 6:57) Volume 1 - May 5
Living God
    (Joshua 3:10) Volume 1 - April 30
Living God and an Everlasting King
    (Jeremiah 10:10) Volume 1 - August 1
Living Stone
    (1 Peter 2:4) Volume 1 - February 17
Living Water
    (John 4:10) Volume 1 - March 15
Long-suffering
    (Alma 9:26) Volume 3 – November 6

Looked upon all the Sereaphic Hosts of Heaven, Before the World was Made
  (Doctrine & Covenants 36:1) Volume 3 – October 21
Lord
  (Matthew 28:6) Volume 1 - October 13
Lord and His Goodness
  (Hosea 3:5) Volume 2 – October 6
Lord and Saviour
  (2 Peter 3:2) Volume 1 - July 7
Lord and Savior Jesus Christ
  (2 Peter 2:20) Volume 1 - December 13
Lord and your Redeemer
  (Doctrine & Covenants 34:12) Volume 3 – October 30
Lord Both of the Dead and Living
  (Romans 14:9) Volume 1 - November 25
Lord, even Alpha and Omega
  (Doctrine & Covenants 54:1) Volume 3 – July 8
Lord Even of the Sabbath
  (Matthew 12:8) Volume 1 - July 24
Lord, Even the Savior
  (Doctrine & Covenants 133:25) Volume 2 – January 1
Lord, for He is our God
  (Joshua 24:18) Volume 1 – August 28
Lord From Heaven
  (1 Corinthians 15:47) Volume 1 - January 12
Lord God
  (Jude 1:4) Volume 1 - August 12
Lord God Almighty
  (2 Nephi 28:15) Volume 1 - April 29
Lord God Almighty, Maker of Heaven, Earth, and Seas, and of all Things that in Them are
  (Doctrine & Covenants 121:4) Volume 3 – March 15
Lord God Almighty, the Most High God
  (3 Nephi 4:32) Volume 3 – April 1
Lord God is my Strength
  (Habakkuk 3:19) Volume 3 – October 4
Lord God of Abraham
  (Genesis 28:13) Volume 1 - July 10
Lord God of Abraham, Isaac, and of Israel
  (1 Chronicles 29:18) Volume 2 – May 3
Lord God of Gods
  (Joshua 22:22) Volume 3 – October 30
Lord God of Hosts
  (Isaiah 10:24) Volume 1 - February 24

Lord God of Israel
(Luke 1:68) Volume 2 – June 19
Lord God of Israel our Father
(1 Chronicles 29:10) Volume 2 – May 4
Lord God of Israel, under whose Wings thou art Come to Trust
(Ruth 2:12) Volume 3 – July 22
Lord God of Israel was their Inheritance
(Joshua 13:33) Volume 2 – October 13
Lord God of my Master Abraham
(Genesis 24:12) Volume 3 – January 3
Lord God of the Inhabitants of Jerusalem, and of the Land of Israel
(Ezekiel 12:19) Volume 3 – December 11
Lord God of our Fathers
(Deuteronomy 26:7) Volume 1 - December 13
Lord God of the Hebrews
(Exodus 7:16) Volume 1 - May 19
Lord God of the Holy Prophets
(Revelation 22:6) Volume 1 - February 6
Lord God of your Fathers
(Deuteronomy 1:11) Volume 1 - August 30
Lord God Omnipotent
(Mosiah 3:21) Volume 1 - June 15
Lord God, the God of Abraham, the God of Isaac, and the God of Jacob
(Alma 29:11) Volume 2 – August 18
Lord God, the Mighty One of Israel
(Doctrine & Covenants 36:1) Volume 2 – December 9
Lord God Who is Almighty
(Helaman 10:11) Volume 3 – May 24
Lord He is God
(Deuteronomy 4:35) Volume 1 - January 10
Lord, He is the God
(1 Kings 18:39) Volume 3 – April 17
Lord in Shiloh
(1 Samuel 1:24) Volume 3 – November 22
Lord is a Man of War
(Exodus 15:3) Volume 3 – April 22
Lord is Above all Gods
(Psalms 135:5) Volume 3 – August 11
Lord is Among Us
(Joshua 22:31) Volume 2 – April 20
Lord is Clean
(Psalms 19:9) Volume 3 – April 26
Lord is God
(Doctrine & Covenants 1:39) Volume 3 – March 7

Lord is God, and Beside Him there is no Savior
   (Doctrine & Covenants 76:1) Volume 2 – December 10
Lord is Good unto them that Wait for Him
   (Lamentations 3:25) Volume 3 – September 30
Lord is Gracious
   (1 Peter 2:3) Volume 3 – February 22
Lord is Great
   (Psalms 135:5) Volume 3 – March 24
Lord is His Name
   (Jeremiah 33:1) Volume 3 – May 1
Lord is in His Holy Temple
   (Habakkuk 2:20) Volume 3 – April 13
Lord is my Helper
   (Hebrews 13:6) Volume 1 - November 10
Lord is my Light
   (Psalms 27:1) Volume 3 – October 24
Lord is my Salvation
   (Psalms 27:1) Volume 3 – December 17
Lord is my Shepherd
   (Psalms 23:1) Volume 3 – February 20
Lord (is) my Strength, and my Fortress, and my Refuge in the Day of Affliction
   (Jeremiah 16:19) Volume 3 – April 19
Lord is Near
   (2 Nephi 7:8) Volume 2 – August 19
Lord is our Judge; the Lord is our Lawgiver
   (Isaiah 33:22) Volume 1 - February 7
Lord is Perfect
   (Psalms 19:7) Volume 3 – April 27
Lord is Pure
   (Psalms 19:8) Volume 3 – April 28
Lord is the Strength of my Life
   (Palms 27:1) Volume 1 - July 16
Lord is the True God, He is the Living God, and an Everlasting King
   (Jeremiah 10:10) Volume 3 – December 31
Lord is their Savior and their Redeemer, the Mighty One of Israel
   (1 Nephi 22:12) Volume 3 – May 15
Lord is their Savior and their Redeemer, the Mighty One of Jacob
   (1 Nephi 21:26) Volume 3 – February 24
Lord is thy Keeper
   (Psalms 121:5) Volume 3 – March 19
Lord is with Thee
   (1 Nephi 17:55) Volume 2 – August 20
Lord is with Us
   (Jeremiah 8:8) Volume 3 – December 28

Lord Jehovah
   (Isaiah 12:2) Volume 1 - August 23
Lord Jesus
   (Luke 24:3) Volume 1 - March 4
Lord Jesus Christ our Saviour
   (Titus 1:4) Volume 3 – May 5
Lord Jesus Christ, the Son of the Father
   (2 John 1:3) Volume 2 – January 4
Lord Jesus Christ their Redeemer
   (3 Nephi 10:10) Volume 3 – May 27
Lord Liveth
   (Jeremiah 5:2) Volume 3 – December 27
Lord, Lord
   (Luke 6:47) Volume 3 – March 8
Lord Mighty in Battle
   (Psalms 24:8) Volume 3 – March 21
Lord my God, mine Holy One
   (Habakkuk 1:12) Volume 3 – April 6
Lord of All
   (Acts 10:36) Volume 1 - October 5
Lord of all the Earth
   (Joshua 3:13) Volume 3 – May 8
Lord of Glory
   (James 2:1) Volume 1 - March 16
Lord of Heaven and Earth
   (Matthew 11:25) Volume 1 - April 28
Lord of Hosts
   (Isaiah 5:16) Volume 1 - September 19
Lord of Hosts is His Name
   (Isaiah 47:4) Volume 3 – January 27
Lord of Hosts is My Name
   (2 Nephi 8:15) Volume 2 – August 21
Lord of Hosts, that Judgest Righteously
   (Jeremiah 11:20) Volume 3 – October 25
Lord of Hosts, that Planted Thee
   (Jeremiah 11:17) Volume 3 – August 27
Lord of Hosts, that Triest the Righteous
   (Jeremiah 20:12) Volume 3 – August 20
Lord of Hosts, the God of Israel
   (Jeremiah 7:3) Volume 3 – November 1
Lord of Lords
   (1 Timothy 6:15) Volume 1 - June 3
Lord of Peace
   (2 Thessalonians 3:16) Volume 3 – May 4

Lord of Sabaoth
(Doctrine & Covenants 95:7) Volume 2 – June 14
Lord of the Sabbath
(Mark 2:28) Volume 1 - November 23
Lord of the Sacrifice
(Leviticus 7:29) Volume 3 – April 4
Lord of the Vineyard
(Jacob 5:75) Volume 1 - June 24
Lord of the Whole Earth
(Doctrine & Covenants 55:1) Volume 1 - June 14
Lord Omnipotent
(Mosiah 3:5) Volume 2 – June 15
Lord our God
(Alma 58:41) Volume 3 – October 12
Lord our God is One Lord
(Deuteronomy 6:4) Volume 1 - January 22
Lord our God, Who has Redeemed us and Made us Free
(Alma 58:41) Volume 2 – August 23
Lord Our Righteousness
(Jeremiah 23:6) Volume 1 - July 17
Lord Strong and Mighty
(Psalms 24:8) Volume 3 – March 21
Lord that hath Mercy on Thee
(3 Nephi 22:10) Volume 2 – October 23
Lord that Healeth
(Exodus 15:26) Volume 1 - February 16
Lord that Maketh all Things
(Isaiah 44:24) Volume 3 – January 24
Lord the God of Heaven
(Jonah 1:9) Volume 1 - April 5
Lord the God of Hosts is His Name
(Amos 4:13) Volume 3 – November 16
Lord the King of Israel
(Isaiah 44:6) Volume 1 - August 24
Lord the Lord and thy God
(Isaiah 51:22) Volume 3 – October 14
Lord, the Redeemer of all Men
(Alma 28:8) Volume 2 – February 16
Lord, the Redeemer of Israel
(Isaiah 49:7) Volume 3 – February 11
Lord, the Redeemer of Israel, His Holy One
(Isaiah 21:7) Volume 3 – January 19
Lord the Righteous Judge
(2 Timothy 4:8) Volume 1 - January 20

Lord, their God, their Redeemer
(1 Nephi 17:30) Volume 3 – May 28
Lord their Redeemer
(1 Nephi 19:18) Volume 3 – January 30
Lord thy God
(Abraham 2:7) Volume 2 – January 26
Lord thy Redeemer, the Holy One of Israel
(1 Nephi 20:17) Volume 3 – May 2
Lord Who Redeemed Abraham
(2 Nephi 27:33) Volume 3 – April 25
Lord, Whose Name is the God of Hosts
(Amos 5:27) Volume 3 – August 13
Lord will roar from Zion, and utter His Voice from Jerusalem
(Amos 1:2) Volume 2 – August 8
Lord your God
(Deuteronomy 10:17) Volume 1 - May 3
Lord your God, even Alpha and Omega, the Beginning and the End, Whose Course is One Eternal Round, the Same Today as Yesterday, and Forever, your God and your Redeemer
(Doctrine & Covenants 35:1) Volume 2 – August 24
Lord your God, even Jesus Christ, the Great I Am, Alpha and Omega, the Beginning and the End, the Same which Looked upon the Wide Expanse of Eternity, and all the Seraphic Hosts of Heaven before the World was Made
(Doctrine & Covenants 38:1) Volume 2 – August 25
Lord your God, even Jesus Christ, your Advocate, Who knoweth the Weakness of Man and how to Succor them who are Tempted
(Doctrine & Covenants 62:1) Volume 2 – December 11
Lord's Christ
(Luke 2:26) Volume 2 – June 17
Lower than the Angels For the Suffering of Death
(Hebrews 2:9) Volume 1 - November 24

M
Made Angels, Authorities, and Powers…Subject to Him
(1 Peter 3:22) Volume 1 – August 17
Made Higher than the Heavens
(Hebrews 7:26) Volume 1 - July 18
Made Lower than the Angels for the Suffering of Death
(Hebrews 2:7) Volume 1 – November 24
Made of a Woman
(Galatians 4:4) Volume 2 – May 7
Made the Earth by His Power
(Jeremiah 51:15) Volume 3 – February 29

Made under the Law
  (Galatians 4:4) Volume 2 – May 8
Maker
  (Hebrews 11:10) Volume 3 - March 31
Maker of Heaven, Earth, and Seas, and of all Things that in them Are
  (Doctrine & Covenants 121:4) Volume 3 – July 9
Maker, thy Husband, the Lord of Hosts is His Name
  (3 Nephi 22:5) Volume 2 – October 22
Majesty
  (Hebrews 8:1) Volume 2 – February 19
Majesty on High
  (Hebrews 1:3) Volume 2 – February 18
Man
  (3 Nephi 11:8) Volume 3 – February 28
Man Approved of God
  (Acts 1:22) Volume 3 – June 16
Man of Counsel is My Name
  (Moses 7:35) Volume 2 – March 30
Man of Holiness
  (Moses 7:35) Volume 2 – January 8
Marvelous Light of God
  (Mosiah 27:29) Volume 2 – December 24
Master
  (Matthew 23:8) Volume 1 - November 4
Master and Lord
  (John 13:13) Volume 3 – June 4
Master in Heaven
  (Colossians 4:1) Volume 3 – January 5
Master of the Vineyard
  (Jacob 5:7) Volume 2 – February 20
Mediator
  (1 Timothy 2:5) Volume 1 - June 29
Mediator between God and Men
  (1 Timothy 2:5) Volume 2 – February 22
Mediator of a Better Covenant
  (Hebrews 8:6) Volume 1 - August 8
Mediator of the New Covenant
  (Hebrews 12:24) Volume 1 - October 9
Mediator of the New Testament
  (Hebrews 9:15) Volume 1 - August 31
Meek and Lowly
  (Matthew 21:5) Volume 2 – March 24
Merciful
  (2 Chronicles 30:9) Volume 1 - September 18

Merciful and Gracious unto Those who Fear Me, and Delight to Honor those who Serve me in Righteousness and in Truth unto the End
(Doctrine & Covenants 76:5) Volume 2 - August 27

Merciful and Faithful High Priest
(Hebrews 2:17 Volume 1 - March 29

Merciful is our God
(Alma 24:15) Volume 2 - August 26

Merciful, O God
(Alma 33:4) Volume 2 - October 3

Messenger of Salvation
(Doctrine & Covenants 93:8) Volume 2 - January 6

Messenger of the Covenant
(Malachi 3:1) Volume 1 - October 10

Messiah
(John 1:41) Volume 1 - October 29

Messiah, the King of Zion, the Rock of Heaven
(Moses 7:53) Volume 2 - January 17

Messiah the Prince
(Daniel 9:25) Volume 3 - May 25

Messiah Who is the Lamb of God
(1 Nephi 12:18) Volume 3 - February 15

Messiah Who Should Come
(1 Nephi 10:17) Volume 3 - February 18

Messias
(John 4:25) Volume 1 - July 12

Mighty God
(Isaiah 9:6) Volume 1 - April 17

Mighty God of Jacob
(Psalms 132:2) Volume 1 - August 7

Mighty One of Israel
(1 Nephi 22:12) Volume 1 - November 9

Mighty One of Jacob
(Isaiah 60:16) Volume 1 - January 7

Mighty to Save
(Doctrine & Covenants 133:47) Volume 3 - July 10

Mightier than all the Earth
(1 Nephi 4:1) Volume 2 - August 28

Mightier than I
(1 Nephi 10:8) Volume 2 - August 29

Minister of the Circumcision for the Truth of God
(Romans 15:8) Volume 1 - February 13

Minister of the Sanctuary and of the True Tabernacle
(Hebrews 8:2) Volume 1 - September 6

More Excellent Way
  (Ether 12:11) Volume 2 – November 11
Most High
  (Acts 7:48) Volume 3 – January 8
Most High God
  (3 Nephi 11:17) Volume 1 - July 9
Most High God, Possessor of Heaven and Earth
  (Genesis 14:19) Volume 2 – August 22
Most High over all the Earth
  (Psalms 83:18) Volume 1 - December 20
My Beloved Son, Which was my Beloved and Chosen from the Beginning
  (Moses 4:2) Volume 3 – March 12
My Deliverer and my Shield
  (Psalms 144:2) Volume 2 – August 17
My Fortress
  (Jeremiah 16:19) Volume 3 – October 28
My Fortress and my Deliverer
  (2 Samuel 2:22) Volume 2 – August 14
My God
  (2 Nephi 4:20) Volume 2 – August 30
My God and my Savior Jesus Christ
  (3 Nephi 5:20) Volume 3 – February 25
My God and your God
  (Moses 6:47) Volume 2 – January 30
My Great God
  (Alma 24:8) Volume 2 – September 1
My Heavenly Father
  (Matthew 15:13) Volume 3 – April 20
My High Tower
  (2 Samuel 22:3) Volume 3 - July 16
My Light and my Salvation
  (Psalms 68:3) Volume 2 – March 16
My Name's Sake
  (1 Nephi 20:9) Volume 2 – September 2
My Refuge in the Day of Affliction
  (Jeremiah 16:19) Volume 3 – October 29
My Refuge, my Savior
  (2 Samuel 22:3) Volume 3 – July 17
My Rock
  (3 Nephi 18:12) Volume 2 – October 18
My Rock and my Salvation
  (Psalms 62:2) Volume 1 - November 14
My Salvation
  (Psalms 27:1) Volume 3 – October 23

My Son
  (Psalms 2:7) Volume 2 – June 4
My Strength
  (1 Nephi 21:5) Volume 2 – September 3
My Strength, and my Fortress, and my Refuge in the Day of Affliction
  (Jeremiah 16:19) Volume 2 – May 9
My Well-beloved
  (2 Nephi 15:1) Volume 3 – March 11

N
Name is from Everlasting
  (Isaiah 63:16) Volume 2 – May 23
Name of Christ, or of God
  (Mosiah 25:23) Volume 2 – September 4
Name of the Lord
  (Genesis 4:26) Volume 2 – May 5
Nazarene
  (Matthew 2:23) Volume 1 - January 30
New and Living Way
  (Hebrews 10:20) Volume 1 - November 27

O
Obtained Eternal Redemption for Us
  (Hebrews 9:12) Volume 1 - September 4
Of Whom are all Things
  (1 Corinthians 8:6) Volume 2 – May 10
Offered Himself without Spot
  (Hebrews 9:11) Volume 1 – July 1
Offering and Sacrifice to God
  (Ephesians 5:2) Volume 1 - September 16
Offering to God
  (Ephesians 5:2) Volume 3 – July 26
Offspring of David
  (Revelation 22:16) Volume 3 – August 8
Omega
  (Revelation 1:11) Volume 1 - November 5
Omegus; even Jesus Christ your Lord
  (Doctrine & Covenants 95:17) Volume 2 – February 21
One
  (Doctrine & Covenants 50:43) Volume 2 – October 15
One Among you Whom ye know Not
  (1 Nephi 10:8) Volume 2 – September 5

One Body
    (1 Corinthians 12:12) Volume 2 – May 11
One Eternal God
    (Alma 11:44) Volume 1 - October 11
One Eternal Round, the Same Today as Yesterday and Forever, your God and your Redeemer
    (Doctrine & Covenants 35:1) Volume 2 - August 31
One Father, even God
    (John 8:41) Volume 3 – April 3
[There is but] One God
    (Alma 11:35) Volume 2 - September 6
[There is] One God
    (1 Timothy 2:5) Volume 3 – August 9
[They are] One God
    (Mosiah 15:4) Volume 2 - September 7
One God and Father of All
    (Ephesians 4:6) Volume 1 - December 3
One God, and One Mediator between God and Man, the Man Christ Jesus
    (1 Timothy 2:51) Volume 1 - August 11
One God and One Shepherd over All
    (1 Nephi 13:41) Volume 2 – March 18
One Having Authority
    (Matthew 7:29) Volume 1 - July 4
One Jesus
    (Acts 17:7) Volume 3 – February 10
One Lord Jesus Christ
    (1 Corinthians 8:6) Volume 3 – April 29
One Mediator between God and Man
    (1 Timothy 2:51)   Volume 3 – August 10
One Messiah
    (2 Nephi 25:18) Volume 2 – September 8
One Shepherd
    (3 Nephi 15:17) Volume 3 – February 17
One with the Father
    (John 10:30) Volume 1 - September 13
Only Begotten
    (Moses 3:18) Volume 2 – January 21
Only Begotten, even Jesus Christ
    (Moses 7:50) Volume 2 – January 24
Only Begotten of the Father, Full of Grace and Truth, even the Spirit of Truth
    (Doctrine & Covenants 93:11) Volume 2 – August 5
Only Begotten of the Father, Full of Grace, Equity, and Truth, Full of Patience, Mercy, and Long-suffering
    (Alma 9:26) Volume 2 – September 9

Only Begotten Son
    (John 1:14) Volume 1 - March 6
Only Lord God
    (Jude 1:4) Volume 3 – April 10
Only Wise and True God, and Jesus Christ, Whom He hath Sent
    (Doctrine & Covenants 132:24) Volume 2 – November 22
Only Wise God our Savior
    (Jude 1:25) Volume 1 - March 9
Our Father, even God
    (John 8:41) Volume 3 - August 1
Our Father, our Redeemer
    (Isaiah 63:16) Volume 1 - November 28
Our Father which art in Heaven
    (Matthew 6:9) Volume 3 – April 21
Our Great and Eternal Head
    (Helaman 13:38) Volume 3 – August 28
Our Great God
    (Alma 24:7) Volume 2 – September 10
Our Life
    (Colossians 3:4) Volume 2 – May 12
Our Lord and Savior Jesus Christ
    (Mormon 3:14) Volume 3 – February 23
Our Lord is above all Gods
    (Psalms 135:5) Volume 3 – March 29
Our Lord Jesus Christ, Who Sitteth on the Right Hand of His Power
    (Moroni 9:26) Volume 2 – November 19
Our Passover
    (Hebrews 13:1) Volume 1 - August 6
Our Peace
    (Ephesians 2:14) Volume 2 – March 26

P
Passed into the Heavens
    (Hebrews 4:14) Volume 1 - February 11
Peace of God
    (Alma 7:27) Volume 2 – September 11
Peniel
    (Genesis 32:30) Volume 1 - November 22
Perfect
    (3 Nephi 12:48) Volume 2 – December 26
Perfect in Knowledge
    (Job 37:16) Volume 1 - December 31

Perfected For ever they that are Sanctified
(Hebrews 10:14) Volume 2 – February 5
Personage
(Joseph Smith History 1:19) Volume 3 – February 27
Personage Whose Brightness and Glory Defy all Description
(Joseph Smith History 1:17) Volume 1 – December 22
Potentate
(1 Timothy 6:15) Volume 3- March 10
Potter
(Isaiah 64:8) Volume 2 – May 13
Power and Spirit of God, which was in Jesus Christ
(3 Nephi 7:21) Volume 2 – October 10
Power Thereof by which (the) Moon was Made
(Doctrine & Covenants 88:8) Volume 3 – September 2
Power Thereof by which (the stars) were Made
(Doctrine & Covenants 88:9) Volume 3 – October 3
Power thereof by which (the Sun) was Made
(Doctrine & Covenants 88:7) Volume 3 - September 5
Precious
(1 Peter 2:7) Volume 3 – August 18
Prepared from the Foundation of the World
(Ether 3:14) Volume 1 - January 14
Prepared…To Redeem My People
(Ether 3:14) Volume 2 – April 3
Priest Forever after the Order of Melchizedek
(Psalms 110:4) Volume 2 – March 13
Prince and a Savior
(Acts 5:31) Volume 2 – January 31
Prince of Life
(Acts 3:15) Volume 1 - January 29
Prince of Peace
(Isaiah 9:6) Volume 1 - October 14
Prince of the Kings of the Earth
(Revelation 1:5) Volume 1 - September 9
[A] Prophet
(Deuteronomy 18:15) Volume 2 – January 12
[The] Prophet
(John 7:40) Volume 2 – May 14
Prophet of Nazareth
(Matthew 21:11) Volume 1 - January 13
Prophet of the Highest
(Luke 1:76) Volume 1 - June 19
Prophet that Should Come into the World
(John 6:14) Volume 3 – May 30

Propitiation for our Sins
    (1 John 2:2) Volume 1 - December 2
Propitiation for the Sins of the Whole World
    (1 John 2:2) Volume 1 - September 24
Propitiation through Faith
    (Romans 3:25) Volume 1 - November 11
Purifier of Silver
    (Doctrine & Covenants 128:24) Volume 3 – November 10
Put Away Sin by the Sacrifice of Himself
    (Hebrews 9:26) Volume 1 - May 22

Q
Quickeneth all Things
    (1 Timothy 6:13) Volume 1 – December 15

R
Rabbi
    (John 1:38) Volume 1 - January 16
Rabbi, Thou art the Son of God, Thou art the King of Israel
    (John 1:49) Volume 3 – June 9
Rabboni
    (John 20:16) Volume 1 - May 6
Raised from the Dead
    (2 Timothy 2:8) Volume 1 - April 3
Raised up out of His Holy Habitation
    (Zechariah 2:13) Volume 3 – September 10
Ready to Judge the Quick and the Dead
    (2 Timothy 4:1) Volume 1 - November 18
Received the Fulness of the Father
    (Doctrine & Covenants 76:71) Volume 2 – November 23
Redeemed us and Made us Free
    (Alma 58:41) Volume 3 – October 13
Redeemer
    (Isaiah 59:20) Volume 1 - September 23
Redeemer and Deliverer from Death and the Chains of Hell
    (Doctrine & Covenants 138:23) Volume 3 – February 5
Redeemer and our God
    (Alma 61:14) Volume 3 - February 9
Redeemer, even Jesus Christ
    (Doctrine & Covenants 80:5) Volume 3 – April 9
Redeemer, even the Son Ahman
    (Doctrine & Covenants 78:20) Volume 3 – January 21

Redeemer is Strong; the Lord of Hosts is His Name
   (Jeremiah 50:34) Volume 3 – September 26
Redeemer of all Men
   (Alma 28:8) Volume 2 – September 12
Redeemer of Israel
   (John 11:25) Volume 1 - November 12
Redeemer of the World
   (Doctrine & Covenants 93:9) Volume 1 - June 25
Redeemer the Holy One of Israel
   (Isaiah 54:5) Volume 3 – February 2
Redeemer, the Mighty One of Israel
   (1 Nephi 22:12) Volume 3 – February 8
Redeemer, Who is Jesus Christ, the Son of God
   (3 Nephi 5:16) Volume 3 – February 13
Redeemer, your Lord, and your God
   (Doctrine & Covenants 10:70) Volume 3 - May 21
Redemption
   (1 Corinthians 1:30) Volume 3 – November 25
Refiner
   (Doctrine & Covenants 128:24) Volume 3 – November 9
Refiner and Purifier of Silver
   (Doctrine & Covenants 128:24) Volume 2 – December 13
Refiner's Fire
   (Malachi 3:2) Volume 1 - August 29
Resurrection and the Life
   (John 11:25) Volume 1 - November 2
Righteous
   (Moses 7:47) Volume 3 – November 23
Righteous art Thou, O Lord
   (Jeremiah 12:1) Volume 3 – October 9
Righteous Branch
   (Jeremiah 23:5) Volume 1 - April 23
Righteous Father
   (John 17:25) Volume 3 – April 15
Righteous Judge
   (2 Timothy 4:8) Volume 1 – February 18
Righteous Man
   (Luke 23:47) Volume 1 - January 3
Righteousness
   (1 Corinthians 1:30) Volume November 23
Roar from Zion, and utter His Voice from Jerusalem
   (Amos 1:2) Volume 3 - July 7
Rock
   (1 Samuel 2:2) Volume 1 - May 7

Rock and mine Everlasting God
(2 Nephi 4:35) Volume 2 – September 13
Rock and their Salvation
(1 Nephi 15:15) Volume 1 - September 14
Rock of their Salvation
(Jacob 7:25) Volume 3 – August 24
Rock from whence ye are Hewn
(2 Nephi 8:1) Volume 2 - September 14
Rock of Heaven
(Moses 7:53) Volume 1 - June 30
Rock of his Salvation
(Deuteronomy 32:15) Volume 1 - May 23
Rock of my Righteousness
(2 Nephi 4:35) Volume 2 – September 15
Rock of my Strength
(Isaiah 17:10) Volume 1 - September 30
Rock of Offense
(1 Peter 2:8) Volume 2 – May 15
Rock of Offense to Both the Houses of Israel
(Isaiah 8:14) Volume 2 – January 15
Rock of our Redeemer, who is Christ, the Son of God
(Helaman 5:12) Volume 2 – March 22
Rock of their Salvation
(Jacob 7:15) Volume 2 – February 25
Rock that is Higher than I
(Psalms 62:1) Volume 2 – January 10
Root
(Revelation 22:16) Volume 3 – August 7
Root and the Offspring of David
(Revelation 22:16) Volume 1 - February 8
Root of David
(Revelation 5:5) Volume 1 - June 23
Round about all Things
(Doctrine & Covenants 88:41) Volume 2 – June 6
Ruler and a Deliverer
(Acts 7:35) Volume 3 – July 12

S
Sacrifice for Sin
(2 Nephi 2:7) Volume 2 – December 29
Sacrifice to God
(Ephesians 5:2) Volume 3 – July 27

Safe Foundation
   (Jacob 4:15) Volume 3 – November 17
Salvation
   (2 Timothy 2:10) Volume 1 - July 22
Salvation of the Lord
   (1 Nephi 19:17) Volume 2 – September 16
Salvation unto the Ends of the Earth
   (1 Nephi 21:6) Volume 2 – September 17
Same, and His Years never Fail
   (Doctrine & Covenants 76:4) Volume 2 – December 31
Same Light that Quickeneth your Understanding
   (Doctrine & Covenants 88:11) Volume 2 – April 1
Same that Spake unto you from the Beginning
   (Doctrine & Covenants 8:12) Volume 2 – September 18
Same Today as Yesterday and Forever, your God and your Redeemer
   (Doctrine & Covenants 35:1) Volume 3 – October 16
Same Unchangeable God
   (Doctrine & Covenants 20:17) Volume 2 – November 24
Same which Came in the Meridian of Time unto Mine Own, and Mine Own Received Me Not
   (Doctrine & Covenants 39:3) Volume 2 – December 15
Same which have taken the Zion of Enoch into Mine Own Bosom
   (Doctrine & Covenants 38:4) Volume 2 – September 19
Same which Knoweth all Things, for all Things are Present before Mine Eyes
   (Doctrine & Covenants 38:2) Volume 2 – December 16
Same which Looked upon the Wide Expanse of Eternity
   (Doctrine & Covenants 36:1) Volume 3 – October 20
Same which Spake, and the World was Made, and all Things Came by Me
   (Doctrine & Covenants 38:3) Volume 2 – September 20
Same Yesterday, Today, and Forever
   (Hebrews 13:8) Volume 2 – March 27
Sanctification
   (1 Corinthians 1:30) Volume 3 - November 24
[Our] Savior
   (1 Timothy 2:3) Volume 2 – May 16
[The] Savior
   (Philippians 3:20) Volume 1 - May 24
Savior and thy Redeemer, the Mighty One of Jacob
   (Isaiah 60:16) Volume 3 – August 2
Savior Jesus Christ
   (Mormon 3:14) Volume 1 - March 23
Savior of Israel
   (Acts 13:23) Volume 2 – March 25

Savior of the Body
 (Ephesians 5:23) Volume 1 - June 5
Savior of the World
 (John 4:42) Volume 1 - April 11
Seed of Abraham
 (Galatians 3:16) Volume 1 - July 11
Seed of David
 (2 Timothy 2:8) Volume 1 - August 26
Seed of the Woman
 (Genesis 3:15) Volume 1 - December 26
Sent that we Might Live through Him
 (1 John 4:9) Volume 1 - October 26
Separate from Sinners
 (Hebrews 7:26) Volume 2 – May 17
Serpent of Brass
 (Alma 37:19) Volume 1 - April 21
Set on the Right Hand of the Throne of the Majesty in the Heaven
 (Hebrews 8:1) Volume 3 – December 7
Shadow of Heavenly Things
 (Hebrews 8:5) Volume 1 - May 21
Shadow of Things to Come
 (Colossians 2:17) Volume 2 – January 2
Shall Appear the Second Time without Sin unto Salvation
 (Hebrews 9:23) Volume 2 – May 19
Shepherd
 (Psalms 23:1) Volume 2 – March 19
Shepherd in the Land
 (Zechariah 11:16) Volume 2 – June 8
Shepherd of Israel
 (Psalms 80:1) Volume 1 - May 25
Shepherd of the Sheep
 (John 10:12) Volume 3 – February 21
Shield
 (Genesis 15:1) Volume 1 - September 27
Shiloh
 (Ezekiel 21:27) Volume 1 - October 12
Sitteth on the Right Hand of God
 (Colossians 3:1) Volume 1 - April 1
Sitteth on the Right Hand of His Power
 (Moroni 9:26) Volume 3 – November 8
Sitteth upon the Throne, even the Lamb
 (Doctrine & Covenants 88:115) Volume 2 – December 21
Son
 (Moses 5:15) Volume 2 – February 1

Son Ahman; or, in other words, Alphus
(Doctrine & Covenants 95:17) Volume 3 – November 13
Son Jesus Christ our Lord
(1 John 5:20) Volume 1 - June 9
Son of Abraham
(Matthew 1:1) Volume 2 – June 18
Son of David
(Matthew 12:23) Volume 1 - March 12
Son of God
(Romans 1:4) Volume 1 - April 8
Son of Man
(Matthew 16:27) Volume 1 - November 1
Son of Man is Lord also of the Sabbath
(Mark 2:28) Volume 3 – February 1
Son of Mary
(Mark 6:3) Volume 1 - December 23
Son of our Great God
(Alma 24:13) Volume 2 – September 21
Son of Righteousness
(3 Nephi 25:2) Volume 2 – October 25
Son of the Blessed
(Mark 14:61) Volume 1 - September 25
Son of the Eternal Father
(1 Nephi 13:40) Volume 1 – May 8
Son of the Everlasting God
(2 Nephi 11:32) Volume 2 – September 22
Son of the Highest
(Luke 1:32) Volume 1 - August 5
Son of the Living God
(Matthew 16:16) Volume 1 – June 16
Son of the Most High God
(Mark 5:7) Volume 1 - October 31
Son, the Only Begotten of the Father
(Alma 5:48) Volume 2 – September 23
Spirit of Jesus Christ
(Doctrine & Covenants 84:45) Volume 3 – March 5
Spirit of Truth
(John 14:17) Volume 1 - June 8
Spiritual Rock
(1 Corinthians 10:4) Volume 1 - June 7
Standard
(1 Nephi 21:22) Volume 2 – September 25
Star Out of Jacob
(Numbers 24:17) Volume 1 - February 1

Stem of Jesse
(Isaiah 11:0) Volume 2 – January 11
Stone
(Jacob 4:15) Volume 1 - August 2
Stone of Israel
(Genesis 49:24) Volume 1 - July 13
Stone of Stumbling
(1 Peter 2:8) Volume 2 – May 20
Stone upon which they might Build and have Safe Foundation
(Jacob 4:15) Volume 2 – September 26
Strength of Israel
(1 Samuel 15:29) Volume 1 - March 22
Strength of the Children of Israel
(Joel 3:16) Volume 1 - January 24
Stretched out the Heavens by His Discretion
(Jeremiah 10:12) Volume 3 – August 19
Stumbling Stone and Rock of Offense
(Romans 9:33) Volume 2 – January 16
Suffered for Us
(1 Peter 2:21) Volume 2 – March 23
Suffered Without the Gate
(Hebrews 13:12) Volume 1 - January 25
Sun of Righteousness
(Malachi 4:2) Volume 1 - February 3
Support
(2 Nephi 4:20) Volume 2 – September 27
Supreme Being
(Doctrine & Covenants 104:7) Volume 2 – February 9
Supreme Creator
(Alma 30:44) Volume 3 – March 26
Surety of a Better Testament
(Hebrews 7:22) Volume 1 - March 17
Swift Witness
(3 Nephi 24:5) Volume 2 – October 24

T
Tabernacle of God
(Doctrine & Covenants 93:35) Volume 3 – August 5
Tasted Death for Every Man
(Hebrews 2:9) Volume 1 - February 20
Teacher Come from God
(John 3:2) Volume 1 - August 16

Teaches the Way of God in Truth
   (Mark 12:14) Volume 3 - November 19
Tempted in all Points as we Are
   (Hebrews 4:15) Volume 2 – March 14
The Man Christ Jesus
   (1 Timothy 2:51) Volume 3 - July 31
There is but One God
   (Alma 11:35) Volume 2 – September 6
There is None other Name given under Heaven save it be this Jesus Christ
   (2 Nephi 25:20) Volume 2 – September 30
There is One God, and One Mediator between God and Men, the Man Christ Jesus
   (1 Timothy 2:5) Volume 1 - August 11
They are One God
   (Alma 22:18) Volume 2 – September 7
This is My Beloved Son, in Whom I am Well Pleased
   (Matthew 3:17) Volume 3 – March 13
Thou art God
   (Alma 22:18) Volume 2 – October 2
Thou art my God
   (Hosea 2:23) Volume 2 – September 24
Thou art the Son of God
   (John 1:49) Volume 3 – December 22
Thou, O Lord, art our Father, our Redeemer; Thy Name is from Everlasting
   (Isaiah 63:16) Volume 3 – January 20
Thou, Whose name alone is Jehovah, art the Most High over all the Earth
   (Psalms 83:18) Volume 2 - May 18
Thy Lord the Lord, and thy God
   (Isaiah 51:22) Volume 3 – May 6
Treasures of Wisdom and Knowledge
   (Colossians 2:3) Volume 1 - September 10
True
   (Matthew 22:6) Volume 3 – November 18
True and Faithful
   (2 Nephi 31:15) Volume 2 – October 4
True and Faithful Witness
   (Jeremiah 42:5) Volume 3 – December 10
True and Living God
   (1 Nephi 17:30) Volume 2 – October 5
True, and Teaches the Way of God in Truth
   (Matthew 22:6) Volume 2 – March 4
True Bread from Heaven
   (John 6:32) Volume 3 – March 6
True Light
   (1 John 2:8) Volume 3 – August 11

True Light that Lighteth every Man that Cometh into the World
(Doctrine & Covenants 93:2) Volume 2 – November 26
True Light, which Lighteth every Man
(John 1:9) Volume 1 - March 14
True Messiah
(2 Nephi 25:18) Volume 3 – May 12
True Messiah, their Lord and their Redeemer
(1 Nephi 10:14) Volume 3 – February 12
True Messiah, their Redeemer and their God
(2 Nephi 1:10) Volume 3 - December 12
True Vine
(John 15:1) Volume 2 – May 25
Truth
(John 14:16) Volume 3 – August 14
Truth of God
(2 Nephi 28:28) Volume 2 – August 16
Truth of the World
(Ether 4:9) Volume 2 – November 8

U
Unchangeable Being
(Mormon 9:19) Volume 2 – November 1
Unchangeable from all Eternity to all Eternity
(Moroni 8:18) Volume 2 – November 18
Unchangeable Priesthood
(Hebrews 7:24) Volume 1 - September 15
Undefiled
(Hebrews 7:26) Volume 3 – December 9
Uphold(s) all Things by the Word of His Power
(Hebrews 1:3) Volume 1 – February 26

V
Very Christ
(2 Nephi 26:12) Volume 2 – February 14

Very Christ and the Very God
(Mormon 3:21) Volume 2 – Octobeer 28
Very Eternal Father
(Mosiah 16:15) Volume 3 – July 14
Very Eternal Father of Heaven and of Earth
(Alma 11:39) Volume 1 - October 16
Very God of Israel
(1 Nephi 19:7) Volume 2 – October 7

Vine
(John 15:1) Volume 1 - March 31
Voice
(3 Nephi 9:1) Volume 2 - November 20
Voice of Lightnings
(Doctrine & Covenants 88:90) Volume 2 - June 1
Voice of One Crying in the Wilderness
(Doctrine & Covenants 88:66) Volume 2 - May 26
Voice of Tempests
(Doctrine & Covenants 88:90) Volume 2 - June 2
Voice of the Day of the Lord
(Zephaniah 1:14) Volume 2 - December 14
Voice of the Lord
(3 Nephi 1:12) Volume 2 - October 9
Voice of the Waves of the Sea heaving Themselves Beyond their Bounds
(Doctrine & Covenants 88:90) Volume 2 - June 3
Voice of Thunderings
(Doctrine & Covenants 88:90) Volume 2 - May 31

W

Way, the Truth, and the Life
(John 14:6) Volume 1 - July 14
Which is, and Which Was, and Which is to Come
(Revelation 1:8) Volume 1 - June 6
Who is Passed into the Heavens
(Hebrews 4:14) Volume 2 - May 29
Who Knew no Sin
(2 Corinthians 5:21) Volume 2 - May 28
Who Shall Judge the Quick and the Dead
(2 Timothy 4:1) Volume 2 - May 27
Wisdom of God
(1 Corinthians 1:24) Volume 3 - August 4
Wisdom, Righteousness, Sanctification, and Redemption
(1 Corinthians 1:30) Volume 2 - March 15
With the Faithful Always
(Doctrine & Covenants 62:9) Volume 2 - November 27
With the Father from the Beginning
(3 Nephi 9:15) Volume 2 - October 12
Without Sin unto Salvation
(Hebrews 9:28) Volume 1 - March 8
Witness of God
(1 John 5:9) Volume 1 - August 15

Wonderful
    (Isaiah 9:6) Volume 1 - January 1
Word
    (John 1:1) Volume 1 - January 21
Word, even the Messenger of Salvation
    (Doctrine & Covenants 93:8) Volume 2 – December 17
Word of God
    (Revelation 19:13) Volume 1 - April 13
Word of Life
    (1 John 1:1) Volume 1 - January 9
Word of the Lord
    (Joshua 22:9) Volume 2 – March 31

Y
Young Child
    (Matthew 2:9) Volume 3 – June 17
Your Father also Which is in Heaven
    (Mark 11:2) Volume 3 – April 18
Your Father, and your God, and my God
    (Doctrine & Covenants 88:75) Volume 2 – May 30
Your Father which is in Heaven
    (Doctrine & Covenants 84:92) Volume 2 – November 28
Your Father, Who is in Heaven
    (Doctrine & Covenants 84:83) Volume 2 – December 18
Your God
    (Moroni 8:8) Volume 3 – December 3
Your Heavenly Father
    (Matthew 6:32) Volume 3 - April 23
Your King
    (John 19:14) Volume 3 – May 29
Your Lord
    (Moroni 8:8) Volume 3 – December 2
Your Lord and your God
    (Moroni 8:8) Volume 3 – February 14
Your Lord and your Redeemer
    (Doctrine & Covenants 34:12) Volume 3 – January 18
Your Redeemer, even Jesus Christ
    (Doctrine & Covenants 80:5) Volume 3 – January 28
Your Redeemer, your Lord, and your God
    (Doctrine & Covenants 10:70) Volume 3 – January 29

Z
Zeal of the Lord of Hosts
   (2 Kings 19:31) Volume 1 - April 12

Additional Name-Titles & Descriptions

Jesus Christ the Son of the Living God, the Savior of the World
  (Doctrine & Covenants 42:1)

Jesus Christ, Who is the Son (Doctrine & Covenants 76:14)

Jesus Christ, Who shall Come (Alma 45:4)

Minute Musings

Spontaneous Combustions of Thought

Volume Two

Appendix Four

A Numerical List of
Scriptural References to Jesus Christ
by Body of Scripture

"That which cometh from above is sacred, and must be spoken with care, and by constraint of the Spirit."
(Doctrine & Covenants 63:64).

compiled by

Philip M. Hudson

References that are used in the three volumes have been selected from the following bodies of scripture:

Old Testament
(221)

New Testament
(415)

Book of Mormon
(257)

Doctrine & Covenants
(181)

Pearl of Great Price
(22)

Bible Dictionary
(2)

Total Scriptural References
1,098

About the Author

Phil Hudson and Jan, his wife of 47 years, have 7 children and over 20 grandchildren. They enjoy whiling away summer days with their family at their cabin, on the shores of Priest Lake, the crown jewel of North Idaho. Phil had a successful family dental practice in Spokane, Washington for 43 years, before retiring in 2015. In his free time, if he and Jan are not visiting their loved ones, he can be found roaming through Pacific Northwest woods, boating on the lake, cycling up mountain passes, riding his motorcycle along forest trails, or snowbiking in winter's deep powder along the Selkirk Crest. He always seems to find the time to write down his thoughts on his laptop, but appreciates Isaac Asimov's frustration when he was asked: "If you knew that you only had 10 minutes left to live, what would you do?" Without hesitation, Asimov answered: "I'd type faster."

Also by the Author

Minute Musings: Volume Two
Minute Musings: Volume Three

Essays: Spray from The Ocean of Thought
Essays: Ripples on a Pond
Essays: Serendipitous Meanderings
Essays: Presents of Mind
Essays: Some Assembly Required

Non-hybrid Seeds of Thought

Book of Mormon Commentary: Born in The Wilderness
Book of Mormon Commentary: Voices From the Dust
Book of Mormon Commentary: Journey to Cumorah

Today, as I Think About my Savior
Daily Inspiration from Scriptural Symbols

Diode Laser Soft Tissue Surgery (Volume One)
Diode Laser Soft Tissue Surgery (Volume Two)
Diode Laser Soft Tissue Surgery (Volume Three)

These, and other titles, are available at online retailers.

www.ingramcontent.com/pod-product-compliance
Lightning Source LLC
Chambersburg PA
CBHW082107280426
43661CB00090B/923